If These Walls Could Talk

If These Walls Could Talk

VICTORIA NECOLE
& 10 TRIUMPHANT WOMEN WHO OVERCAME ABUSE

IF THESE WALLS COULD TALK
Published by Purposely Created Publishing Group™
Copyright © 2018 Victoria Necole Long
All rights reserved.

No part of this book may be reproduced, distributed or transmitted in any form by any means, graphic, electronic, or mechanical, including photocopy, recording, taping, or by any information storage or retrieval system, without permission in writing from the publisher, except in the case of reprints in the context of reviews, quotes, or references.

Printed in the United States of America
ISBN: 978-1-949134-37-7

Special discounts are available on bulk quantity purchases by book clubs, associations and special interest groups. For details email: sales@publishyourgift.com or call (888) 949-6228.
For information log on to www.PublishYourGift.com

This book is dedicated to the little girls that were told "no one will believe you," " if you tell then I will kill you and your family," "no one will love you the way that I do," or "you will only be worth what's between your legs." We are here to tell you that you are not what they said. No one will ever hurt you again. God loves you more than you will ever know. Your story is your truth, and no one has to believe you but you.

Table of Contents

Introduction 1

Chapter 1: There's a Boogeyman in the Dark
Miyoka Chehron.. 3

Chapter 2: Breathless
Brittaney Pleasant 13

Chapter 3: Shattered but Not Defeated
LaShun Thrasher 25

Chapter 4: Sheltered Soul
Lola Sterling 35

Chapter 5: Past Failures to Future Greatness
Kenyetta Cheatum 45

Chapter 6: Pretty Beast
Kerscelia L. Patterson 55

Chapter 7: Mother, May I?
Star Washington 67

Chapter 8: No Fairytale Love
Shaniqua Davis 75

Chapter 9: He Loves Me, He Loves Me Not
Melissa Morehead 87

Chapter 10: Face the Facts
Jamie Oliver 99

Chapter 11: Do You Really Know?
Victoria Necole 111

Sources 121
Meet the Authors 123

Introduction

Courage, strength, and determination are the qualities that will be revealed to you by each of the 11 women who have come forth to share their stories. Each storyline is unique, yet they are all similar. Similar, you say? They are similar because they all cover taboo subjects that are rarely discussed but are experienced frequently. The stories include such topics as domestic violence, sexual, verbal, and emotional abuse, and bullying. In each of the stories you are about to read, there is level of fear and hurt that each of these women had to overcome.

According to the National Domestic Violence Hotline, "one in four women (24.3 percent) aged 18 and older in the United States have been the victim of severe physical violence by an intimate partner in their lifetime, and nearly half of all women have experienced psychological abuse by an intimate partner in their lifetime." Perpetrators use bullying and sexual harassment as techniques to damage another individual, and according to Bullying Statistics, verbal bullying is the most common amongst adults. Think about those statistics for a moment. Now either you or someone you know has been a victim of domestic, sexual, or verbal abuse. Something to really think about, huh?

As you will find after reading the stories of each of these brave 11 women, many cases of abuse are not reported during the time they are experienced. Confusion, fear, abandonment, hurt, shame, embarrassment, and disappointment are just a few of the feelings that prevented each of these women from sharing their experiences in the past. Furthermore, they show that it wasn't the end for them, but only the start of something greater. Each story demonstrates a sense of triumph and victory for each woman as they overcome their victimizer and show that they are no longer victims.

Follow each of these women on their journey and witness them regain control over their lives and speak up and out against abuse while showing other women that they are not alone.

These 11 brave women are no longer broken but experiencing a breakthrough!

There's a Boogeyman in the Dark

MIYOKA CHEHRON

Where do I began? What is my story and how do I tell it when I've lived in this silence about it for so long? I was a little girl at the time. I guess my most recent memory of everything is from when I was around six or seven. I didn't even know back then what good touch and bad touch were, but over the course of my childhood, I experienced things that no child should ever encounter.

My childhood is filled with many memories. There are the normal memories of playing with my sisters and my friends, going to the movies, and definitely hanging out at the mall. Most of my memories are of a pretty normal household and engaging in regular activities, like going to church and family functions. However, my most vivid childhood memories are of him fussing about something and having something negative to say. He would purposely be hurtful behind closed doors.

I guess I'd never really considered myself a victim. I knew what happened to me was wrong, and even worse than that, I felt like something was wrong with me because as I grew up, I never really found myself wanting to be intimate or close with anyone. I have always loved the idea of love and having someone to protect me, but to allow someone to get close enough to hurt me? Absolutely not. I hated the thought of someone touching me in any form. I knew the reason why, but to admit to myself that I had been victimized was harder than actually being victimized. I'm not sure when it started or when it ended, but what I do know is that for years, I was a victim. I never really thought about it that way growing up. I just knew that what was going on with me wasn't right.

When I was little, I would hear stories of the Boogeyman. He would come out at night and attack the bad children. I thought he lived under my bed and in my closet. I was wrong. I remember sometimes late at night, I would wake up, and I could tell that someone had been in my room. There was no evidence that the person was there, but I knew they had been there, lurking in the dark, waiting for me to fall asleep. I won't say his name, or even give a description, but late at night, he would slither into my room like the snake he was, and he would lie there on the floor until he knew I was asleep. At first I didn't know that he was there, but once I was asleep, he would crawl to the side of my bed, slide his hands up under the sheets, and fondle me. There were even some mornings when I would wake up and my private area would be sore and I could barely move. It was in those moments that I could tell that I had been touched. He never talked to me or let me know he was there. He was always a shadow. I started to pretend to be asleep to catch him. I would wake up and ask, "Why are you in my room?" There was always a reason why. "Oh, I thought I saw something" or "Oh, I was checking something." There was even a time when I noticed him outside the bathroom window watching me.

I thought that if I covered myself up as much as possible, whether it was with extra sheets, blankets, or clothing, I would be less likely to "provoke" the monster to touch me again. I would dress in layers, even in hot weather. Others would always ask why, and I would always lie, saying "I'm cold" or "I don't like dress gowns." I was scared out of my mind to tell anyone. What if they didn't believe me? What if that angered him and made him do worse things to me? I hoped keeping my mouth shut would show him I was willing to be silent forever so that he would stop. But he didn't. He would give me looks during the day to let me know that I better not say a word. No place was safe. He was always there. The fondling and watching violated my innocence.

Then I thought to myself, "Well, he didn't penetrate me, so maybe nothing happened. Maybe I just did something to myself. Maybe my body is changing and that's why I'm sore." Then I started sleeping with shorts on. When I woke up, there would be a rip in my shorts. It didn't stop.

My offender played the role of a father in my life, and therefore I was forced to do things with him and my family. We would go to church, and I would watch him talk about God—about how people needed to live a life that was a representation of God. Funny thing, though, watching him put on a show didn't make me draw away from God. Instead, it pushed me closer to him. It made me crave God as a father like never before. It made me pray harder. It made me feel like if I lived a certain way, God would fix everything, and everything would stop. However, it didn't change anything.

When I spoke of it, I hated the day I opened my mouth. I wasn't prepared for the questions that were constantly asked of us. "Did you make it all up?" Really? Why would I do a thing like that? However, I knew why the questions were asked. At the end of the day, I was a child, and they didn't believe me. All the pastors and counselors we told believed us. We weren't really sure why our family didn't. I felt bad for taking my family through this grief to the point that I said it never happened and that I made it all up because I didn't like the person. I chose to focus on how this would affect my family, and soon I forgot about myself. I felt like I was left in the dark.

As time went by, I was filled with numbness and unbearable pain, but I masked it well. I only allowed people to see the devoted daughter or the good student. I was filled with so many emotions I had never known existed. There was an emptiness that was so hollow. The older I got, the more I felt like a zombie giving the illusion of someone living. I felt isolated in a crowded room and lonely most of the times, but no one knew because I was the funny one, always making people laugh. I always had a smile on my face and always appeared happy. I sat in silence broken on the inside, confused about who I was, and afraid to trust or love.

For years I walked around feeling shameful, thinking everybody could see my past if they looked close enough. Although he didn't hurt me physically in the sense of him penetrating me, he laid the groundwork for who I became and for what I became when it came to whom I would allow to enter my life. I slept with the lights on until my early thirties. Darkness represented secrets, deception, and pain. To say I was afraid of the dark was an understatement. It was not because the dark in and of itself of which I was afraid, it was my abuser.

I used to tell myself that at least I didn't go through what other people had gone through. Nonetheless, I endured something that affected me in more ways than I ever knew. When I got older, I started to desire a meaningful and long-lasting relationship with someone who I did not feel was going to violate or hurt me. Yes, I still have some trust issues but I'm working through them daily.

When I was 20, I met a young man, and I made the decision to marry him. I guess I just kind of jumped in head first. We got married on my 21st birthday. I didn't know anything about being a wife. I had not dealt with my issues, and boy did I struggle. I didn't want to be touched, looked at, or even in the same room as him. It's not that he did anything to me, but I was still dealing with my issues from my past that had never been dealt with. Having sex was too painful, and it reminded me of the hurt I had experienced in my childhood. I was wounded, and my scars were starting to bleed.

I had a negative attitude when it came to sex. I deemed it as something that took my power away as a woman, something that made me smaller than my partner. I had no self-esteem, and I was sinking into depression. I really thought that if I got married, the pain of my past would be behind me, and I'd be just fine. But I wasn't, and the pain was infecting my marriage. I was young and immature, and unfortunately, I didn't know how to handle matters at all during this time in my life. I made matters worse because of my inability to know how to really work through my issues.

My husband wanted to be close to me, but I couldn't handle any sexual closeness. I eventually told myself that I just had the wrong partner, and that nothing was wrong with me. Our marriage ended in divorce, so now not only was I broken, but my marriage and my children's family life as they know it were also broken.

I remarried, but the pain didn't leave. The shame became one with me and the loneliness grew. The pain was immeasurably worse in my second marriage than in my first because now there was someone "new" trying to get close to me. I started to grow bitter at God because I was broken, and I felt like he refused to fix me and make me whole. I was hurting and didn't know how to make the pain stop.

In the midst of my pain, I was raising two children, trying hard to make sure that they never felt my pain, never experienced what I went through. I smothered them, always kissing and hugging them, always telling them they were smart and worthy. I gave out hugs and kisses when they were hurting. I babied them to the point of handicapping them. But once in a blue moon, I also had these moments where I was short tempered with my kids and said some things that I probably regretted later. I was unbalanced in every area of my life, damaging my spouse and my children.

I remember crying out to the Lord, asking him to help me not to hurt others because I was hurting. It wasn't until I moved to Radcliff, Kentucky, and started attending a local church that healing started to truly take place. I needed to begin the process of deliverance and healing. I forgave everybody for choosing my offender's word over mine. I even forgave my offender for what he did, even though he never apologized or took responsibility for his actions. Most importantly, I forgave myself.

God started to speak to me in a way that made Him more real in my life than He had ever been. He assured me that he would never leave me nor forsake me and that if I was open to walking with Him, I would be healed, and I would assist others during their journey as well. He showed me that I struggled over the years due to unforgiveness, which was like poison destroying my relationships and family.

I learned how to go to a safe place and seek the Father there. I learned to give Him my pains, my disappointments, and my hurts. I learned how to allow Him to make me whole through Him.

My journey has not been an easy one, and although it has been very painful along the way, I am grateful to God for it all.

My past no longer holds me hostage or weighs me down to the point of feeling dragged around in my life. I am healed, and I am whole. I no longer feel separated or alienated from God. Everything in my life has changed for the better, and I'm continuously walking in my healing.

There are many other Boogeymen still out there hurting innocent children. I'm not sure how you stop them, but my desire is that no one ever has to be afraid of the dark or afraid to speak up and say, "This is happening to me." I've learned how to not allow myself to live in shame of what happened, because it wasn't my fault. I was a child. I'm no longer scared of my Boogeyman, because once I found my voice I took his power away. I confronted him once I was older, and I told him that I knew what he had done to me, and that it was wrong. That he was wrong. Children are supposed to feel safe, not afraid. He denied it, of course, but that's okay, because I walk in forgiveness. I can forgive, but I most definitely will never forget. I wonder how my life would have turned out if I had never been sexually abused. Would my marriage have survived? Would I have raised my children differently? What would I have been like if I hadn't known this hurt, this pain? Maybe I will never truly know, but I am glad that I have found peace through a loving Father in my Savior. I realize that the monster didn't win, because I'm stronger than I ever thought I would be. I am no longer afraid to turn the lights out and go to sleep. I'm the one with all of the power because I make the choice in how my story ends, and it is in victory.

Breathless

BRITTANEY PLEASANT

I had just finalized my divorce from my husband of all of one year. We were separated eight months into the marriage, and I had just found out I was pregnant with my first child. All of this after meeting him at a job I was working. I was 19 years old, and although I attended high school away from home, this was my first time really being free to make my own choices and do what I wanted with no adult supervision. Truth be told, I should have run after our first conversation on the phone. I remember us talking and laughing, and suddenly, he started yelling and calling me a bitch and hung up the phone. He called right back and swore he wasn't talking to me when he said that and asked why I hung up. It was very odd to me, but I brushed it off, and we continued with our relationship. Things only got worse after that. It got to a point where I couldn't even walk to class without him swearing another guy was trying to talk to me as I walked by swarms of people between classes. When I didn't answer my phone (while I was in class), he would go ballistic and start accusing me of sleeping around on him. Still I stayed. Finally, he gave me an ultimatum—either I drop out of school or we would have to break up. Of course, I did the most reasonable thing—I left school to be with him, and on my 20th birthday we got married. You are probably wondering where my parents were and why they allowed me to get married at such a young age—and to a guy I had only met three months earlier. You see, even though he was verbally and emotionally abusive and very controlling, I was still looking for love. To be honest, I was in love with the idea of love, and I would do anything to have it, even if that meant risking my relationship with my parents and other family members who supported me. I essentially traded my family for one that didn't really care for me at all. My ex-husband's family couldn't understand why I, a "stuck-up college girl,") wanted to be with a boy who didn't even graduate high school. But I didn't care. All I knew is that even in all of the dysfunction, he made me happy, and I wanted nothing more than to be with him. I think a part of me was still holding on to the dream that so many little girls have of growing up, getting married, and living happily ever after. Of course, my relationship was far from perfect, but I believed we just had to "work out the kinks." I was a very intelligent girl who had all the book sense in the world, but I was as green as grass with no common sense at all when it came to relationships and dating. On top of that, at this point in my life, I was very rebellious. I was very sheltered growing up, and attending a public boarding school as a teen robbed me of the "normal" life and dating experiences my friends back home got to enjoy. I was a "late bloomer" in many ways, and I would pay for it dearly. It was with my experience with my ex-husband that planted the seeds for the way my relationships would continue to go, not because it was their fault, but because I failed to take the time to evaluate myself, learn from my mistakes, and heal from the past before jumping into another relationship. After the divorce, I was happy (for the most part), single, and ready to mingle. I was lonely, vulnerable, and still very naïve. I still couldn't grasp why things ended the way they did. One part of me said forget him and move on, while another part of me was still holding on to the good memories that we had wishing things could have ended differently (or not at all).

I was looking for love to fill the void that I had, and I started dating a guy whom I will call Jason. He was new to town. He and his family moved to Alabama from Chicago to escape the violence in the city. He was everything I thought I wanted at the time—a "bad boy" with the persona, swagger, and reputation to match—you know, the baggy jeans that sagged off his butt just right, fresh Js. And although he was cool as a fan, people knew to never cross him because he also had a bad temper. We met at work, and after a few casual conversations and exchanging phone numbers we were talking on the phone all day almost every day. I ended up developing a wonderful relationship with his family and would chill with them almost every day after work. I was totally infatuated with his charm and the fact that I just felt safe with him, and before long, I moved out of my parents' house, got my own place, and invited him to live with me and my son. Stupid, I know. But hey, hindsight is definitely 20/20. A couple of months into the relationship, he started to become really controlling, but he was smart enough to make it seem as though he was being protective of me, so it was a turn on. We had been dating for about four months and everything was perfect until…

WHAM! I reeled backwards from the blow he dealt me and hit the floor. Before I knew it, he was on top of me with his hands around my throat.

"You think you better than me bitch? I told you, you ain't nothing without me!" he spat angrily. The room around me was spinning. I was kicking, squirming, and crying, trying to beg him to release his grip. I became more breathless and lightheaded with each attempt to free myself, and the room slowly faded to black as I started to lose consciousness.

I wanted to give up. I was tired of fighting. I didn't understand what I had done wrong. After the fourth month, something inside him just snapped, and he started beating me. It was also during this time that he started drinking heavily. Even though he was a diabetic, he would drink a bottle (or two) of Aristocrat vodka almost every day. It bothered me, but whenever I tried to object, it would lead to another fight, so I started leaving him alone about it. He would always ask me, "B, why do you keep making me do this to you?" Of course, I apologized and always felt like somehow, I brought everything on myself. Instead of those kisses and touches of adoration and affection, the fights and the verbal, emotional, and physical abuse started to happen often. Again, I should have run, but I chose to stay. I stayed because a part of me believed that love really does conquer all, and maybe, just maybe, one day he would realize the pain he was causing me and change. I stayed because I thought I could literally love the hell out of him. I stayed because I actually loved him more than I loved myself.

   I would often miss days from nursing school, seeing my parents, and work to hide the scratches and bruises. I later found out that my dad knew about the abuse the entire time. We were close, and he always had sort of a sixth sense when it came to me trying to hide things. So, he came and got my son with no questions asked. Of course, I wanted to run into his arms and tell him everything that was happening, but I tried to handle it on my own. I thought about leaving several times, but when I did, he threatened to kill not only me, but my family as well. Part of me was tempted to call his bluff because I was tired of living in this hell, but a bigger part of me worried that he might really be serious, and I would never be able to live with myself if something happened to my family because of a choice I made. I was also sure that if I prayed enough and if I loved him hard enough, he would change. On top of that, his fits of rage were unpredictable. It seemed like he just knew how to reel me back in every time I got close to my breaking point and started to plan my exit strategy. He would of course apologize and swear it would never happen again. (Even though I never really believed him, I held on to a glimmer of hope that maybe this time he really would change). Then, he would start doing everything he did when we first met—the sweet good mornings, the kisses, late nights playing video games together—but things always went back to the way they were—the days and nights I dreaded when I walked on egg shells because I could never tell what mood he was going to be in. It was a never-ending cycle. Even through all of that, never once did I realize that he wasn't for me, so no matter how much I prayed for God to change him and help him to love me, he never would, and in trying to love him, I had forgotten to love myself and remember my own worth.

The Breaking Point

As I lay on the floor, slowly feeling the darkness surrounding me I thought, "Lord, I give up. I'm tired. If there is something better for me, if I need to leave please give me a sign." I looked up into his face, and he was silent, looking down at me with a mask-like sinister grin on his face. I closed my eyes and let my body relax. "This is it. This is how it's going to end," I thought as I felt his grip tighten around my throat. All I could think about was my son. After begging my dad to let him spend the night with me, he finally gave in with a look that told me I better get myself together and nothing better happen to his grandbaby.

"No! No! Get off mommy!" I opened my eyes to see my two-year-old running towards us.

"Get outta here lil nigga!" he snarled. With one hand still on my throat, he got up and with one swift blow he backhanded my son. Rage filled me, and a new strength that I had never known found its way into my body as I watched my baby slide across the living room floor.

I ran to him, picked him up, and grabbed a knife that was sitting on the counter. I must have looked wild and nothing like the quiet, timid girl he was used to seeing because he just looked at me as I ran past him and locked my son and myself in the bathroom. I dropped the knife and stood there rocking my son, crying silently. He beat on the door until he gave up and decided to go to bed. I waited another hour to come out of the bathroom before I crept out to find him sleeping peacefully in bed. Any other night, I may have sat there staring at him, afraid to go to sleep and contemplating taking his life before he took mine. But that night, I quietly packed all my clothes in garbage bags and decided the first thing in the morning I would tell him my son and I were leaving to go do laundry and I was never coming back to this house. I sat there until the sun came up, praying and crying. I cried because I was grateful both of us were alive. I cried because my baby had been my lifesaver and my guardian angel at the perfect moment. I cried because my son had been subjected to all of this because of my selfishness. I cried because I finally realized I was worth so much more and I was not willing to accept less. My time had been wasted, but a lesson had been learned, and I was grateful that through it all, God loved me enough to pick me up out of the darkness just when I had given up hope. It certainly wasn't by my own strength that I overcame this situation. It was all due to God and the grace and mercy He decided to extend to me during a time I needed Him the most.

Ironically, I found my relationship with God during this time to be just as rocky and emotional as my relationship with Jason was. I have always had strong faith in God, and my goal has always been to love people like He loves us. Somehow within all that, I forgot that I still can't love someone else more than I love myself. I would pray for Jason to change and pray that God would show him how to love me. When things continued to follow the same cycle, I became angry with God, as if I was not responsible for the pain and turmoil I was going through. I put up Bible verses all over the house. I told God that I trusted Him and asked Him to give me signs and wisdom on what to do, and when He did, I ignored Him and continued to try to do things my way. Still, He kept me.

Lessons Learned

No matter how much you may feel that getting into another relationship may help you to heal, take time for yourself to breathe, reflect on things, forgive, and learn how to love yourself before you try to give your heart to someone else. Still being in a broken place when entering a new relationship can cloud your vision and prevent you from having the relationship that you deserve, and if you're not careful, you will be willing to accept love that isn't love at all. You simply cannot hope to build a future if you refuse to let go of painful pieces of the past.

As grateful as I was for my son's presence that night, he should have never been subjected to anything like that. Although he was only two at the time, seven years later, he still remembers that night. When you have children, you're not allowed to be selfish anymore. Be careful who you allow into your children's lives because you never know what lasting effect it may have on them.

I grew up within a household where I wasn't allowed to do what I wanted all the time. If my parents felt something was unsafe or could get me into trouble, they said no, and that was the end of it. I looked at it as them simply being controlling, but it was true love and protection that I learned to appreciate later in life. When I got into relationships later on down the road, I looked for that same love and protection, but what I was receiving was nothing more than insecurity and control. Be careful that you don't confuse the two.

Many people say love doesn't hurt. That's not at all true. It does hurt. It is inevitable in any relationship. Sometimes it may come from hearing the truth about yourself or someone saying something out of anger during a heated argument. What you must be careful not to do is to confuse abuse with love. Abuse or control is never a reflection of love. Someone who loves you will not continue to do anything that breaks you down. Don't ever continue to try to breathe life into a situation that constantly leaves you breathless.

Perhaps the biggest lesson I learned is that prayer only works when you're willing to truly listen and submit to the will and voice of God. This was one of the most painful experiences in my life, but to be honest, it didn't have to be. Even without a spoken prayer, God is always listening, watching, and guiding along the right path, but how many of us have ignored the warning signs and kept right on going into the "danger zone"? I blamed God so many times for not turning things around when I was just unwilling to obey Him. I didn't realize that sometimes the biggest gift is in the goodbye. This is not only true for the victims of abuse, but for the perpetrators as well. Sometimes it takes them seeing a glimpse of God through you and realizing what they lost to make them turn their lives around. If not, the best thing to remember is that it is not our job to "fix" anyone. God is more than capable, and He will never make you compromise your value, your worth, or your sanity to do it.

Shattered but Not Defeated

LASHUN THRASHER

It was fall of 1993. I was hanging out with my friend Cassie at her house. She was having a big barbeque. It was pretty hot outside, so we walked up front and sat on the front porch. While we were talking, this tall, good-looking guy walked over and immediately caught my attention. He was brown skinned with straight white teeth, he had beautiful hazel eyes, and you could tell he worked out often. We locked eyes as he walked up, sat beside me, and introduced himself. He asked if we could exchange phone numbers. From that day on, we became inseparable. He seemed perfect for me at first, but I learned quickly that this relationship was going to be hell.

Two months into the relationship, I started to notice his attitude change. He became really controlling, possessive, and jealous over me. We had our good and bad days. One particular night started off well but took a turn for the worse. We went out to eat, and everything was going fine. We headed back to his place and had a couple drinks and hours of passionate sex. He did things to me that I had never experienced before, which explained why I was so addicted to him and put up with the abuse. When we finished, we fell asleep until I heard a loud banging on the door around 2 or 3 a.m. I woke Damon up and told him to answer the door. When I got dressed, I overheard a female saying, "Let me in!" and what sounded like her trying to snatch the screen door open. I tried to leave. The girl went crazy trying to bust my car windows out with a brick, so he wrestled with her. I was ready to pull off but was stopped because my passenger door flung open. He jumped in the car with me, saying, "Take off! I'll tell you where to turn." I switched seats with him, and he drove like a bat out of hell, swerving all over the road, running over curves, and running the red lights while I was going off on him. I was so mad because that was the night I found out he was cheating on me. I was crying and screaming at him, telling him to get out of my car. That's when he hit me in my face! I felt his hands on the back of my neck squeezing really hard while he was gritting his teeth saying, "Bitch! Shut the fuck up!" My mind was racing. He had just hit me, my neck was hurting, and I couldn't get my keys. I sat there crying so hard and shaking like a leaf because I was scared he was going to hurt me. That was just the beginning of the physical abuse.

It was the summer of 1994. I got my own place a few houses down from my mom. It was small, but I was excited because it was mine. I was young and living life but depressed because I'd gained so much weight since Damon and I began to date. Damon was still physically abusive. He was so angry at me because I didn't move in with him. I was cooking one day and he had gotten dropped off, so we had a nice lunch, watched a movie, and lay around relaxing. Someone knocked on my door. I went to see who it was, and it was some guy looking for someone else. I told him he had the wrong place and that I believed he was looking for the house in front of mine. He said, "Okay thanks" and left. I closed the door and went back to lie down and cuddle with Damon, and before I knew it, he was straddled over me with all of his weight, choking me while I was wrestling to get his hands from around my neck. I couldn't breathe, and he didn't let up. He kept saying, "You cheating on me now, huh? You cheating on me!" I begged him to get off of me. He was hurting me, and I couldn't move. His weight had me in one spot on my back. All I could do was kick my feet and move my arms and hands. I tried to scream, and he put his hands over my mouth. I had to bite him and put my fingers in his eyes to get him off of me. When he got off, I jumped up as fast as I could and tried to run to the door, but he snatched me back by my arm and I fell back against the bed. I had a tall, thick stand-up mirror in my bathroom, and the door was wide open. I don't know how I did it, but before I knew it, I remember pushing him away from me and he went back into that mirror. It shattered everywhere. He was on the floor with his arms in the air. I was scared because I saw blood, and he didn't move. I thought I'd killed him. "Oh lord, I don't want to go to jail for murder!" I thought. I was holding my throat so tightly that it was hurting. I didn't know if I should help him or run. I walked towards him and he reached his hand out for me to help him up. I hesitated for a second but helped him up and assisted him to the daybed to sit down. I was so stupid because when I think about it, this man had just tried to kill me, and I was helping him. I got some towels and cleaned up the blood that was on him, got some of the glass out of his skin and hair, and cleaned up the broken mirror all over the floor. He put his shirt on and had me drop him off at home because he had to get ready for work. When I got back, I walked over to my mom's house to lie down. She asked me why I was so quiet. I said I didn't know and just lay there thinking that if I took some pills, then I would die quietly. I just wanted out. I started ignoring Damon and telling him I had to work mandatory overtime because we were short staffed. I had even started parking my car two to three blocks away from my house and acting like I wasn't home. I kept this going on for months, which irritated him, but I stayed close to my family.

I didn't tell them what was going on, but I did tell my best friend since second grade, Rita, when I went over her house one day. I remember her inviting me over so we could go out to eat and do some shopping. When we sat down to eat, I told her everything that was going on in my relationship with Damon and how he was abusing me. She was in shock. She said, "You better get away from him, girl, before he hurt you really bad or kill you!" I told her I was scared of him and that I couldn't tell my family because the men in my family didn't play, and I didn't want anyone to get hurt or go to jail. She responded, "And your point is? I don't get it. I would tell them anyway so they can protect you. Girl, you better get some help or start calling the police on him or something because he's dangerous." I told her I found out through one of his friends that he was on crack. His friend was going off on him when he came over to their house one night. They were outside arguing, and his friend said, "Man, all I want is my money you owe me, and we good. I hooked you up with a deal, man. I could have sold that crack to the dude up the street. My man had the money, but you my boy, so I was trying to look out for you. And now you want to play me. I'm giving you until tomorrow evening around this time to get my money." I was so in shock and scared. I wanted a relationship so badly, I never did my research to see what type of man he really was. My friend kept trying to warn me to leave Damon alone, but I didn't want to listen. At the end of November, I had been talking to my auntie who lives in Florida. She wanted me to come live with her. She'd help me get a job at the hospital where she worked and offered me a place to stay until I got on my feet. I was excited thinking that this might be my way out.

On December 19th, 1994, my mother was in the hospital having my baby brother. I was mixed with emotions because I was planning to leave for Florida the following week. I was with two of my cousins leaving the hospital, and when we were walking out the door, I heard Damon call my name. I looked back and saw him running in my direction. I turned around to run but felt a hard hit in my back and almost fell. My cousins turned around and asked me what happened. I told them I was okay, but my ankle was hurting. They were ready to fight in the middle of the hospital.

They were so upset, yelling, "We'll fuck his ass up right here and now!" I was able to convince them to let it go, so they helped me up, and we started walking to the car. When we got to the car, Damon jumped in the backseat. He was twisting the skin on my right arm so hard but was acting like he was kissing me so they wouldn't see me crying until I pushed him away from me. My cousin who was driving asked, "LaShun, what is he doing to you?" Damon responded, "Why I got to be doing something to her?" My cousin said, "She's not crying for nothing!" and they began to argue. Before I knew it, he opened my door. He had my face hanging out of the car and was trying to push me out. I was trying to hold on to the back of the driver's seat and screamed. My cousin hit the brakes and got out, pulling him out from the passenger side of the car. Damon got jumped that night. My cousin told him to walk, but I begged her to drop him off at his house, and she did. I knew then that I had to get away from him. He was getting worse than ever. My cousins said they wouldn't tell anyone about that incident.

My aunt called a few days later and asked if I was still coming. I told her "no"—that I wanted to stay and help my mom with my brother. I could tell she was disappointed. I think now I was more scared of leaving my family behind because I'd never been that far away from home before. I soon started going to church. Sunday mornings, evenings, and Wednesdays for Bible study, I was there. I enjoyed going to church because it was family oriented. I invited Damon a few times, and when he went, he wasn't at all into it. It's bad when your presence is a bother to those around you. People knew Damon, and his reputation wasn't great. I was embarrassed about how he would act when things didn't go his way. He would have bad temper tantrums, punching his hands, slamming doors, and just acting stupid for no reason. I started reading Psalms and The

Book of Timothy, and I found myself getting stronger in certain areas of my life. I was really building a prayer life with God, and I would be so amused when he answered my prayers right before my eyes. I would pray, "Lord, thank you for all you've done for me and my family. I'm so grateful and continue to work in my life." I started to pray that my feelings for Damon would go away and that I would let go and move on with my life.

In March of 1995, I called my second uncle Frank and asked him if I could stay with him at his home in Muncie because I missed living there and was bored where I was currently living. I kept praying and asking the Lord to give me the strength to leave. I talked to my mom about it. She said, "Are you sure you want to go back?" I told her I wanted to start over and get away for a little while and that I was breaking up with Damon. She said, "Okay. He has a nasty attitude. I'm glad you leaving his rude tail." I got tired of being treated badly. I told my pastor I was moving back to Muncie with my family because I was in a bad relationship that was stressing me out, but I couldn't go into details about it.

I was with Damon one night at his mom's house. He said he was ready to go because she was fussing at him about something in the other room. So we went to his place. He fell asleep, so I cleaned up and left. The next day, he called me several times and told me to come over and hurry. When I arrived, he walked up to me and gave me a kiss, but the stern look on his face was throwing me off. I asked what was wrong. He said, "You threw my dope away when you cleaned up last night!" Then he had grabbed me from the back of my head and pulled my keys, so I bit him. He said, "I'm sorry. I love you." I was out of breath and crying. He hugged me, and I held on to my keys to make sure he didn't take them. I looked up, and he had closed the front door, walked over to me, and started kissing and undressing me. I went along with it so he wouldn't fight me anymore. When he fell asleep, I got my few personal items from the bathroom and the few outfits I had hanging in the closet, eased out to the car, and left. I broke up with Damon, and I wanted to leave before he tried to stop me. I left and went to my mom's house because I had moved out of my place and started staying with her. I packed some of my belongings and told my family I was leaving that night, and if Damon called, they didn't know where I was staying. They understood. I took what I wanted and got on the road. It was a 30-minute drive to Muncie. I called my uncle, and he let me know where he left the keys for me. I prayed, praised, and cried to God because the hardest thing in the world to do was leave this guy with whom I was crazy in love but of whom I was terrified at the same time. But I thought he was going to kill me, so I knew it was time to go. I did miss him, but I got a job and was working. I got over him slowly. It took a lot of prayer and trusting God for me to get out of that toxic relationship, but I had faith, and He led me through. I finally let him go and moved on with my life. I felt relieved, I had peace and got my joy back. I found myself again!

Sheltered Soul

LOLA STERLING

Through the window, I gaze to see the birds flying free in the sky, only to wonder what their freedom feels like as they soar to the top of the tree branches. Some gracefully soar and lead the way. As always, there's that one bird that is within the group but alone, and yet that doesn't stop their ability to keep going. (That would be me.) I've always had a fascination with birds, bees, butterflies, and squirrels because nature was my best friend. The winds spoke to me and the heaven showed me pictures as I laid my sheltered soul hidden in the woods from danger's hand. Because here in this place, I was safe—safe from that touch that changed the course of my life, my thinking, and eventually, my ways. I was only eight or nine years old lying in my cozy bed when it began. He would teach me to use my lips to caress his body. I was so confused and sad, yet I smiled, because then maybe, just maybe, he'd remember I was just a child. Oh how I wished not to return to that bed behind that wall where I knew eventually he would awake. I cried many days but learned at an early age to keep secrets. I became the best-kept secret ever. I'll never forget watching *Donahue* approximately a year or so later. The episode was about molestation and rape. That's where I got the idea to tell.

There were nights and days when I smiled but screamed through my eyes, only to hope someone would hear my cry. I was constantly bombarded with questions like, "What were you doing that made your uncle or aunt want to kiss, fondle, and supposedly have sex with you?" If these accusatory statements were not painful enough, I was told by those who sexually preyed upon me that I looked at them sexually. That I sat on their laps. Their insults were never ending. I internalized these statements and I told myself, all this sexual and physical abuse was my fault.

I knew it was wrong and I knew he knew it was wrong. Wasn't he supposed to love me, teach me, and protect me from the real animals in the world? Yet he would visit my room at will or call me to his. I felt like I was having an out-of-body experience when my uncle abused me. Before long, my aunt, who I thought was supposed to be my friend and loved me, also started abusing me.

I floated from one place to the next, and everyone seemed to have the same idea about me. So I started having the same idea about me too. I'll go into more detail in a minute. I couldn't tell anyone else called family or friends and become a greater disappointment. They found out anyway, and we had the talk and that talk led to another devastation. I then found myself living in a psychiatric hospital due to a failed suicide attempt and a scattered brain that was in pain but had no voice. I tried. I tried to tell, and then yep, I got into trouble. So much trouble it was. My parents were very sure to always tell us about diseases and how they would eat our bodies away. They would say, "Don't be so fast, and stay out of people's faces. In my heart all I wanted to do was scream "I did!" and tell them everything, but—I always had a but—but I don't want to cause trouble, but I didn't do anything, but they're not going to believe me anyway. I ran away more times than one could count. I was depressed, yet I was only nine or ten or eleven. The numbers get all mushed around in my head, but that was me and my sheltered soul laying in those beds, bathrooms, floors, cars, and vans. Since telling the first time around didn't go so well, I ran and tried to tell someone else. So, you want to know what happened!?! I was abused again and at the hands of my aunt and uncle, who were supposed to be my protectors. They put objects inside of me, and it hurt, and yet in the sexual acts, I had false orgasms, and that confused me more! I didn't understand why my body would respond in such a sexual way when what was being done was evil. In my transition from one house to the next and sleeping with both males and females, sex became such a routine that when it didn't happen, I asked for it.

Now, I was truly crazy, but who could I turn to? Who would believe me? I wasn't going to tell anyway after being threatened. So, the happy little girl that I was within slowly started to die. He lay next to me to console my tears, at least I thought, but somehow his penis was in me and on me, and my tears just joined in where the others already flowed. As time passed on, so did I, right into the hands of another abuser, and she was a woman. It was like a movie—he went out, and she came in. As crazy as it sounds is as crazy as I felt. As life happened, this became my not-happy happy norm.

I took upon that sexual spirit that I learned to entertain at a very young and tender age. I went from being sexually abused to becoming sexually promiscuous. I thought if I learned how to sexually make someone happy, then they would really love me. I finally made the decision to be touched myself, and I chose a male friend I went to school with and liked. When I was abused at home, I would call him so that in my mind, his hands would be the last hands that touched me. Anywho, round and round we went, and then I slept with whom I wanted, and they slept with me. I was raped. When I said "No," anger, brokenness, and hate flooded my being. I cried behind closed doors and smiled with a distant eye to all those around me. So many days and nights, I wanted to just run home and lay my head on my own mother's lap, but states away she lived, and I was a ward of the state and alone. This couldn't be life. This couldn't be all there was for me to see. I wanted to hate, I wanted to kill, but my heart only cried and felt sad for the ones who tampered my body. I hurt so deeply because of what they did, and I even tried to pray, but my foster family and I went to so many churches like they got paid for it, and I had no clue what to say or to whom to say it. I knew beyond the distant sky someone was up there looking down on me. Although I was angry about all the abuse I had endured, I realized that God sheltered my soul.

Some people shy away from sex and or make other choices in life because of the abuse they endure. Abuse made me an abuser of myself and my body. I became addicted to sex like drugs.

So, there is a small snippet of my life for which I'm more than thankful today. I'm thankful because although the enemy tried to take me out, twist up my mind, kill me, devastate my dreams, and derail me from transforming as a beautiful butterfly, Abba had His hand upon me the entire time. My sheltered soul was awaiting the day that I would begin my journey from the promise to the manifestation, and that's what you must also do. I appeared not to be listening as I sat in the back pew watching the clock and mimicking others, but the Word was speaking to me in a different way. A few years later as a teen, I finally gave my life to Christ with some understanding, and the first thing that I worked on was forgiving myself and the others who wronged me.

"For if you forgive other people when they sin against you, your Heavenly father will also forgive you." —Matthew 6:14, NIV

I had to begin with me. This has been a long process, but it's easier today than the first day I had to look myself in the mirror and acknowledge I didn't have control over my flesh. I was blessed that I had not contracted any diseases. I had consensual and non-consensual sex so many times that there could have been two of me. When I was young, this Bishop said to me "I thought you were going to save that for me," not knowing or caring about my history. But God, He kept sending His Angels to speak to me, to live next door to me, to work on my job and prophecy to my soul. The Bible was always my friend. I just didn't have the right tools to use it properly. I kept fighting for me and started again and again forgiving myself and then others. See, forgiveness isn't about them, it's about you. It's about shifting gears and staying still as healing becomes your friend. I learned much later in life my healing took so long because I was scared to get help and reveal the depths of my pain and trust again. As well, I had to learn to trust me, I would pick up feelings or feel a magnet-like pull towards those who had the same illness as I did. Yes,

I said illness, and because I was still weak, I failed. I failed big! I stayed down for a minute, but my desire to please God was greater than anything I had ever known, and the peace I felt was worth fighting for, so I got up and fought for me. It meant daily I had to decide that I was worth it—that what The Bible said about me was true.

"'For I know the plans I have for you,' declares the lord, 'plans to prosper you and not to harm you, plans to give you hope and a future.'" — *Jeremiah 29:11 NIV*

This is what I wanted to believe. This is what I was chasing, and the only way to do it was to know the Lord. Yes, there were times I asked, "Why me?" This old lady told me many moons ago that I may not ever know the answers to my questions, but she believed that somehow, someway, someday, it would all work together for my good.

I believe that at some point we must find the moment where we accepted that it was okay to be treated in such a manner and the pain became pleasure. Find the day that our heart lost touch with reality and believed the lies we were told. Perhaps it was the first day or the third year, but there was a day. Pulling every lie out of my head and filling it with words of courage, strength and dignity became important. I wanted to match the smile on my face that I was known for. I wanted to be loved like the love I still freely gave and yet no one knew. I just wanted to protect and serve with kindness those from whom others had walked away because they didn't understand that their mental instability came from the hands of those they loved. I believe if we allow God to truly use us, the very thing that tried to take us out will be that which we help others with. It still amazes me how through trial after trial, failure after failure, excuse after excuse, He still came to see about me.

Where does life begin when so much seems to been lost? It begins with you! It begins with one believing and making the choice to live. It begins with you saying, "Today, I begin again." You can start over at anytime, and please don't think it's too late or you're too old. If you allow bitterness, anger, hatred, stubbornness, sadness, or defiance to maintain a lock on your heart, then those who wronged you still have control over you. I know it's not the easiest thing to do, but facing the mirror and saying, "Today is the day I make the choice to start over and forgive" releases you from the control of the enemy. You will still be faced with life's obstacles, but daily knowing that I have God on my side and a host of angels upon whom to call made fighting much easier. You can overcome the hurt, the pain, the insecurity, the instability, and the depression by knowing that "Greater is He that is in you than he that is in the world" and believing it. Put the Word to work, say what you see until you see what you say, and do it in the name of Jesus Christ, because His name means something. It makes some stuff shake, rattle, and roll. Begin to look at the glass as half full instead of half empty, shattered instead of broken, at peace instead of in pieces. It's time to wake up that butterfly in you, come out of the cocoon, and see the beauty that you truly are!

I will never say to anyone "Get over it!" I will say, "You have to make a choice." It's so much easier to trust when you know who really has your back! I know that God has my back! Although at one time I blamed Him and cursed Him, I did not know Him. He still covered me, and I'm so grateful. There is beauty in your ashes, and only God can go and take what people thought was no good, rendered useless, and dead and restore it. Isaiah's remnant idea carries hope for restoration. The day I stopped walking confined and imprisoned was one of the greatest days of my life. Forgiveness breaks the chains of bondage and breaks through self-imprisonment and self-sabotage. It leads to a life of stability, which affects everyone around us, so you have to make a choice to win. When you win, everyone wins. Look closely in the mirror and see the winner in you. Say, "I forgive you" and say the name of someone you want to start with. First pray for guidance, freedom, and healing. I rejoice with each and every person who gets free knowing that the worst is behind them. It is an awesome place to be. This means that right now is a new beginning. No matter how many I have had, I'm moving forward realizing that my voice has a sound, and to the ears of those who love me and to God, my voice matters. I matter. Elijah had a simple, straightforward prayer rooted in his relationship with God: " I am your servant." This is how I want God to hear my voice and trust my walk because I came to make a difference and simply be me! I truly hope and pray that something I said helped someone and helped to make a difference in your life. I hope you made the greatest choice today to give God another chance and forgive.

Everything has worked together for my good, and I'm still evolving to become someone's miracle, be a blessing to those I meet daily, and have a clean heart with clear and good intentions. My greatest desire is to please the one who created me, and I call Him Abba! He has given me beauty for my ashes, and He will do the same for you!

Be blessed, be unique, and always be you!

Past Failures to Future Greatness

KENYETTA CHEATUM

Puberty kicks in and causes young women to feel like they are not beautiful or less attractive than others. Some young women develop faster than others. My story begins like most girls who are silently going through, have gone through, or will be going through that identity crisis of finding their voice and/or simply a place of belonging. I can remember one day, I was putting on my clothes for work when my daughter came home from school crying. She was upset. She began to say to me "Mama, I want to talk to you. I want to be like you. I want to be beautiful. I want everyone to like me." And at that moment, her words stopped me in my tracks. I began to ask her what she meant, because in my eyes, she's always been a beautiful young lady. It was then that I learned about the confrontation that had happened at school. She began to tell me about this little girl who had been picking on her because she was bigger in size. The little girl had been calling her fat. The little girl also went as far as to tell her that she was ugly and would never amount to anything. As I looked at her, I was so hurt because she didn't love herself due to what someone thought or said about her. I saw the pain in her eyes from going through this incident. My beautiful daughter began to tell me that she did not want to live and wanted to quit school. I told her that she was only in the fifth grade, and quitting wasn't an option. I reassured her that sometimes people can be mean and rude. I also told her that no matter what, she would always be my beautiful princess.

I was so hurt witnessing my own daughter having to deal with bullying issues. I was also bullied, but never to the extent that my child was facing at this time. I was always picked on about my clothes and shoes. My mother, who had worked hard to take care of me, taught me to be appreciative of what I had or what was given, whether new or old. I never had the finer things in life, but I never went hungry or lacking in clothing or shoes. I was also bullied because of my weight, but never to the extent that my daughter was. I tried to fit in. I began to beg for friendship, even to the point of trying to buy my friends just to say they were my friends. So when I saw my own daughter experience any type of bullying, it really hit close to home. My granny raised me off a saying that sticks and stones may break my bones but words will never hurt me. When you sit and think about it, though, words do really hurt.

Watching her go through this and trying to remain humble and help her was so hard because I was her protector.

Because of the pain I saw my daughter encounter, I began to brainstorm and think of what I could do to help motivate and encourage my daughter to never be afraid of who she is and what she will become. I started thinking about how I could gather other females like her together to encourage, motivate, and build up one another. At that moment, the idea of Big Sistas with Purpose (BSWP) was formed. BSWP is an organization that was created to fight against bullying and low self-esteem in little girls and plus size females. We are here to be that listening ear for the communities, churches, and schools. We are here to provide support and find ways to overcome and cope with bullying, self-esteem, and confidence issues.

I had a close friend and partner listen to my ideas when it first came to me. Little did I know, my idea made enough of an impression on him that he spoke to a marketing company. I got a call from a marketing company called Hairston and Brown Consulting Agency of Birmingham, Alabama. A lady by the name of Mrs. Brown gave me feedback on what I needed to do to get started. She helped me to establish BSWP. Mrs. Brown said that she believed in my vision, and she told me in front of my grandmother that she didn't know how it was going to take, but she knew that one day it would be a success. The words that Mrs. Brown spoke gave me the strength and the encouragement that I needed to move forward with my dreams and goals as a business owner.

When I left her office, I felt like I had accomplished the most I ever had in my life other than graduating high school. I now was a business owner. Although BSWP was formed and established, little did I know about the unexpected odds that I would soon face. Months later, my mother became ill. It began to take a toll on me and the goals I had planned for the organization as well as my personal life. It was 4 a.m. on Sept 3rd, 2011 when I received a phone call from the hospital stating that my mom had passed away.

And at the time, I began to feel bad and wanted to give up on it all—my life, school, and the organization. I felt like I had lost my whole world. Two months later, my baby daughter lost her father on my mother's birthday. I began to think, "What else could happen?" At that point, I felt worthless as a mom because I had to explain to my daughter that she wasn't going to able to see her father anymore. From this point on, nothing even mattered to me.

My first cousins were planning a trip to the beach and asked me if I wanted to go. So I decided to go. That was the best decision I ever made. There was an overcoming spirit that calmed me from the moment that I stepped foot and took my first breath on the beach. That next morning when the sun was rising, I sat on the balcony. I looked up and saw a perfect silhouette of my mother in the sky. I heard her say, "Kenyetta, you must get yourself together for you and your girls. I am fine and no longer hurting or suffering. It's time for you to live your life and take care of your babies." That moment was like a breath of fresh air. I believe that this was a closure point for me to let me know that she was okay and that I could move forward with my dreams and goals. It was also closure because my girls needed me as much as I needed them. This conversation has played in my mind over and over again to keep me motivated and moving forward.

I came home from the beach and decided to enroll in school. My goal was to go to school to get a degree in business. Although it has its ups and downs, I am still currently enrolled. Since the beach trip, I decided to put things in perspective concerning BSWP. So I put together an annual plus-size model show for BSWP. This show allows the members and participants to gain self-confidence and boost their self-esteem. I also started having meetings to discuss business for the group, to keep in touch with them, and to talk about any new issues that may have come up. BSWP opens a forum and creates a platform for the girls to be able to discuss things that they otherwise feel uncomfortable to speak about on a normal basis due to feeling alienated and picked on. It also allows them to express their feelings among others who are experiencing or have already experienced the same or similar incidents.

My oldest daughter is now a teenager, and her trials and tribulations have begun to grow all over again. She began questioning her worth and purpose here on earth. She started hanging with the wrong people. Her personality and attitude around us changed. She began arguing with her sister a lot and trying to run away from home. She was verbally abusive to me and others. It was as though she was possessed by a demonic spirit. I began to question my ways and what I was doing wrong as a parent. I began to reach out to my father and grandmother for guidance. I was so lost and hurt. I began to think of prayers and started praying over her life and motivating her. I gave her scriptures to read and even reached out to close friends who had been through some of the same things that she was going through.

Then my journey of bad health began. Everything that I thought could go wrong went wrong. I began to allow my self-esteem to fall. I began to feel like I wasn't good enough to be a parent. I became depressed and always stressed. I thought about what others said about me. I was so weak at this point. I could not even be there mentally and physically for myself, let alone for my kids. My health was slowly declining. I was diagnosed with high blood pressure, diabetes, high cholesterol, and sleep apnea. All these illnesses were causing me to get sicker than normal. I was hospitalized for weeks at a time.

I remember that day when the doctor told me that I was about to have heart attack or stroke. This was an eye opener for me. I began to take life more seriously. I began to exercise and watch what I ate. But none of these changes were good enough. I began to think that maybe I was just supposed to be like this. At that point in my life, I needed more encouragement than ever. My friend, who was a plus size model, told me about the plus size pageant system. I immediately became interested. I registered, and boy was it an experience of a lifetime. Never in a million years did I think that I would be a pageant queen. There were ladies of all shapes and sizes from all over the state of Alabama, and we all had one thing in common—we were all beautiful and uniquely made. With this move, I was able to promote my BSWP brand, which stands against anti-bullying, promotes self-esteem, and raises one's self-confidence. However, because I felt that the other women around me were drop-dead gorgeous, I started feeling unconfident about myself.

As I embraced the experience, I learned that the Miss Alabama Plus America Pageant system wasn't about just beauty, but about building one another through all types of trials and tribulations. The Miss Alabama Plus America Pageant system as a whole was about a sisterhood that is stronger through prayer, dedication, and support from one another.

I can remember this one young lady who prayed with me. Her mother even cried as she prayed for me. Although I did not get a chance to go to nationals, I loved the fact that I had the chance to represent my city for the year. I remember when I was sick the Queens of the Miss Alabama Plus America Pageant system came and surprised me at the hospital.

These are just a few examples of the love we experienced. While I in the process of competing in the pageant, my daughter started getting seizures, and we couldn't figure out the cause. At this time, I really couldn't think of the competition. My mind was only on her.

Things finally started to come around. In 2017, I competed again in the Mrs. Category. By this time, I was sure to do my best being newly married and having the support of my husband, my children, and my family. I had also gained a new confidence from a recent weight loss surgery. This time, I won first runner up, which meant the world to me, because I had never won before. There are many things that I went through, such as losing my mom, losing my daughter's father, trying to lose weight, failing in school, being talked about and misused, and being denied success while trying to elevate my career, dreams and goals. I even questioned myself as a mother and a business owner. However, if I had to do it again, I would not change these struggles.

Although it hasn't been an easy road, I found out who I am and my purpose in life. I realize that I have goals and dreams to accomplish, and I won't stop until I have reached them. There are two scriptures I quote faithfully. The first is Proverbs 31:25: "She is clothed with dignity and she laughs without fear of the future" (NLT). This scripture alone is motivating and powerful to me and has helped me become more successful than ever before. Though I faced many issues, I never stopped going forward. I refused to give up. There were times when I thought I was not going to make it because I lost things and friends I thought I needed in order to be successful. But the truth of the matter is that it all was a learning process called "growth."

The second scripture I often quote and live by is I Thessalonians 5:18: "Give thanks in all circumstances; for this is God's will for you in Christ Jesus" (NIV). No matter what came my way, I knew that it was God who kept me from hurt, harm, and danger. It was nothing but my faith that kept me from giving up. When I praised Him in spite of what I was going through, I became blessed. I thank Him for all that I have been through because it has made me wiser and more knowledgeable, and in that, I can truly stay humble of the many blessings.

So no matter what it looks like, always remember to give thanks and praise Him in advance for the overflow. I believe you should always pray without ceasing (I Thessalonians 5:17). Never give up on yourself, but motivate yourself. "So as the body without the spirit is dead, so faith without works is dead also" (James 2:26, NKJV). It was never about what I didn't have, but about having the smaller things that become greater. Remember to write the vision and make it plain (Habakkuk 2:2)—no excuses; no regrets. No one else's opinion matters. Love yourself, and all else will fall into place. I am not a statistic, but a woman of faith, courage, dignity, and power. I am not my statistic because I did not let my past negative issues hinder my growth. I have overcome my situations with prayer and dedication to Christ Jesus and self-evaluations. As a good friend of mine, Victoria Long, says, "Affirm yourself daily." If I hadn't kept the faith and continued to pray throughout my storms, I would not be where I am. Romans 8:28 states, "And we know that in all things God works for the good of those who love him, who have been called according to his purpose" (NIV). I know that my vision became my provision, but I would not be able to do any of it without the help of the Lord ordering my steps. As always, keep him first in all that you do and acknowledge him, and he will direct your path.

Pretty Beast

KERSCELIA L. PATTERSON

I marvel at the fact we are equipped with these innate senses alerting us to danger. Remember when you felt the hairs stand up on your back or neck? Or the uneasy rumbling or sinking feeling in the pit of your stomach? Your sixth sense is supposedly there to give you intuitive awareness while the other five senses of taste, touch, smell, hearing, and sight may not be in use at the moment. However, with all these faculties in place, you may still walk into harm's way, corrupt business partnerships, or ministries where false doctrine is being sold and preached. Your senses are "sniffing out trouble or danger," and yet there are others who run to the nearest safe heaven and humbling themselves to say, "I need help."

When you sniffed trouble, what did you do? No, really? Think back for a second to that moment. Did you learn from that event? Did you get on the hamster wheel like a many of us? The hamster wheel is the mindless running in circles, continuing the same cycle of life choices until something or someone comes in our line of vision. When these moments come, they only distract us enough to flee the wheel for a while. Then we get right back onto that squeaky wheel called "trouble."

I'm curious about when you or that friend had a first date with the person you met online. Be honest! Did you sniff trouble? Did you chalk up your feelings as "overreacting"? Did your friends assume your standards are just too high? Did you push those warning signs aside and say, "I will give this a chance." Your family and friends read your inner thoughts about being nervous on the most trending social media being developed at this second. Are you or were you sniffing out troubling? You tell me.

Trending in the news today: cadaver sniffed out a body of a person looking to simply meet a nice person. That body is yours. Yes, the one who refused to listen to every warning sign when your sixth sense sniffed out trouble. We must remember, a person can do everything right, and natural anxiety mimicking unwarranted fear can slide into the dynamics. However, evil is out there, sniffing ways to be diabolical and a predator on society as well.

If you did not know, fail to recall, or want a word of encouragement, rest assured that God or your higher power equipped you with tools to sniff out trouble. You may have your spiritual angels or the gift of discernment. We have been left with the Holy Bible or any resources you utilize to keep you spiritually renewed, replenished, and equipped during your mediation and or devotional time.

If These Walls Could Talk

This new journey is a cautionary tale when sniffing trouble. I can't make this up, because I lived it.

"I'm friends with the monster that's under my bed. Get along with the voices inside of my head you're trying to save me, stop holding your breath and you think I'm crazy, yeah, you think I'm crazy." —Eminem, 2013

Who in the world can forget the year of 1992, let alone the summer? Mary J. Blige's chart-popping hit *What's the 411* set it off for getting ready to head out for the night parties. Other popular hits included *End of the Road* by Boyz to Men, *Baby Got Back* by Sir Mix-a-Lot, *Jump* by Kris Kross, *Tears in Heaven* by Eric Clapton, *My Lovin' (You're Never Gonna Get It)* by En Vogue, *Diamonds and Pearls* by Prince and The New Power Generation, and *Remember the Time* by Michael Jackson. I'm about to jump out of my skin. There are many songs stirring up this girl's memories of freedom, fun times, liberations, and coming into self.

The 48 hours of girl time was the great getaway any hard-working college sophomore required, right? I loved looking into my rearview mirror as I saw that campus of Western Kentucky University shrink in size. Ugh, I felt like a kid running away from home every opportunity I had. Louisville, here I come.

I made it to Louisville. I could see the silhouette of movement in my girlfriend Shawnee's fab brownstone. I adored her place, however, she kept it looking like a complete utter mess. We found ourselves cleaning it up the next morning, which is a story for another time. Wait—now that I think about it, I think Shawnee was suckering my girls and me in. She was always asking all five of us to help. Now I'm pissed as I reflect back. Hey, when you stay somewhere for free, you just help out. But you will learn that literally everything comes with a cost.

Knock! Knock! The door opened. Music was blaring one of the top 100 hits of 1992, and everyone knows Louisville, KY radio stations back then were the best. Of course, I greeted my girls with, "You guys are in full party mode!" "No, girl, we were waiting on you and the rest of the crew!" was the reply. You have to understand, not only did I attend college, I worked and came from a middle-class black family. There was and is pride in the historical aspect of the legacy I was carrying. It was nothing for my father to hand me a roll of cash during a visit. However, I connected with females who did not work and hustled, prostituted, boosted, shoplifted, and dated one of the biggest drug dealers in the city. Another college girlfriend of mine was terrified of them, and yet she associated with them, even against her will at times. Strange creatures we were.

I know at least someone had a little change to get marijuana. Trust me, if they had weed, someone sold some food stamps. I saw enough of their hustles to write a *How to Get Over for Dummies book*. So, I was money for liquor. The heavy hitter was the drug dealer's girlfriend, Riha, and she rolled in when she wanted. Riha had to decide what she would wear—mink in the summer (yes, I said mink), gold, and diamonds for all her fingers. She had a real "grill"—all gold teeth—not the "pull-outs" like they wear today. I waited for no one. However, we were a crew, and I really thought she was unique, features and all. Now we could speed up the process for the pre-party if we could just go to the drug dealer's and Riha's house. The snag was that he despised all of Riha's girlfriends in the crew except me and the other college girl. Well, this threw a nasty twist into the circle because he made it clear we were the only two allowed in his home.

With Riha's permission, we snuck into the drug dealer's house when he was not home. These girls were frequent users of cocaine and crack, which were considered to be recreational and not hidden at parties. Nevertheless, they had more time on their hands during the week, so I did not know their real frequency of use. Well, since we were in the drug dealer's and Riha's apartment, one of the girls looked down and realized tons of smalls balls of cocaine had dropped onto the carpet from regulating baggings and sorting. Shawnee, NeNe, and Katie were on their hands and knees collecting these tiny balls until they had enough and they were able to cut it up and snort lines. They offered Riha a hit. She was repulsed. "Are you kidding?" she blurted out. "Why would you pick up that from the from the ground when I have my own personal stashed?" she asked as she blew smoke in slow motion from her cigarette. I laughed as I sipped my wine. They looked pathetic. Image the scene of hyenas on your local nature channel mauling a rotting carcass. Their rotting carcass was the crumbs of cocaine on a carpet, and they were squabbling not to take too much.

Riha and I evaporated like ghosts to her bedroom, where she sprinkled out a few white lines of cocaine for us to share. This is a sign of a bond or a sign to get you hooked for another potential customer. "Hurry up!" she said. "They are greedy and I don't want them to have any." We cleaned up the glass and then topped it off by rubbing the residue over our gums for additional kind of an aphrodisiac. "Where were you two?" her sister NeNe yelled out. Did I not mention a minor detail? Oh yes! Her sister is the "alleged" prostitute whom the drug dealer despises the most. Everywhere we go, every man wants to know why we are with NeNe. It took me a while to figure out why men were asking us until a guy came right out and told me. Enough said!

Well, it was time to get dressed, because we wanted to be out on the scene by 10:00 p.m. or 11:00 p.m. Tequila shots were flowing—I'm not a big fan of tequila—and they were chatting "eat the worm" to everyone. Gross! I was not eating the worm. I think that worm stayed in that bottle that night. Shawnee was rolling up joints for us to share. That is what we did. We shared everything. We were a crew. NeNe was cooking up crack cocaine to sprinkle on the marijuana. It was my first time watching the process. The smell sent chills down my spine.

You must be wondering how in the world how in the world I was running with one of the top drug dealers and associates and how so much illegal activity was happening in every direction. We were not worried about law enforcement because we had an inside connection who would call if we needed to be on the high alert or if Riha's boyfriend should lay low. It was that simple to us back then— we knew we were protected.

Everyone was at the apartment looking flawless, video-shoot ready, hair perfect. Back then, you lined your lips with a chocolate or black liner and put some gloss in between to try to make your fake mole look real and hit the top club scenes. Tonight was different. We were going to a motel party, which was very common in Louisville. You usually got out when the sun was about to come up. Envy, drunkenness, and orgies make up these parties. I warn you, as

I warned you before, that those who do such things will not inherit the kingdom of God (Galatians 5:21).

Well, if you had asthma, then that room was no place for you to be. We walked in like bosses. The air was thick with the aroma off marijuana, and I mean thick. The lights were out except for the one, which lit up the sink in the blue-painted room with double beds. It was packed with quite a few females. I don't remember many guys. In fact, I only remember one guy. Anyway, there were plenty of cocaine over by the sick, groups chatting it up smoking joints on the beds, and free-flowing alcohol. I think this was truly girls' time. It couldn't get any better than this with your girls.

Although Katie was tipsy, she was rather skittish and sticking close to me. Katie whispered in my ear, "Don't leave me alone in here." "I won't," I replied. Katie was interesting. She did every drug and drank everything but was fearing something. While we were chatting it up, I could see in my peripheral vision NeNe slipping into the bath with some dude. At first I thought she was so greedy trying to score free drugs. I couldn't stand her, and she hated me. However, I had to be somewhat tolerant because Shawnee was our mutual friend. NeNe was steadfast in destroying my relationship with her younger sister Riha.

"Katie, I can't hold this any longer. The bathroom is free. I have to go use it. Hold my drink."

Another rule when you are with your crew is that you don't set your drink down. You have a friend hold it. Off I went. I locked the doors. I didn't trust those people. I used the bathroom, freshened up my lip gloss, combed my perfect, cold, black, Hallie Berry-style hair back in place, and steadied myself. It was show time again.

I unlocked the door to make my dramatic entrance and looked up in slow motion. There was not a single soul in the room! I was alone in the bathroom for a few minutes, and an entire room was cleared out!

This thin-framed black male sat smoking a joint with the red tip illuminating when he inhaled in the dark corner. It was lucky for me that he was smoking, simply for the fact that this helped me pinpoint his location. Instantly, every danger alert bell was ringing. They were sounding earlier, but I was drowning them out with drugs and alcohols. I coolly asked, "Where did my friends go?" "They left," he replied. "Do you mind taking me back to my friend's place?" I asked him. "Who do you think is going to pay for all the shit you and your girls snorted, smoked, and drunk up? That's my shit?" "Well, I did not know anything about this arrangement, I don't know what you are talking about." According to the thin man, NeNe performed oral sex on him, but that still did not settle the entire debt. He thought she was too disgusting to have sex with. Go figure!

I don't know if being high and drunk distorted my perception, but I felt as right then that all my body organs were going to betray me. This thin man's mannerisms were odd, to say the least. He slowly walked over near one of the double beds. In a low, deep, baritone voice, I heard him say, "Lie down." I was trying to use every street credit of calmness I could muster. "Please, I don't know anything. Please don't do this." My mind started racing, remembering all the fights I would get into in school. As I stood there gazing at the silver .38 auto Smith & Wesson on the nightstand, I wondered if all that fighting was going to help me in this fight for my life?

Decades later, I physically become ill as I did that night when this man told me my friends left me there and said I was to pay the debt—in other words, have sex with him or whatever he desired to do with me. He pushed me back on that bed, and I remember I fell back in slow motion. He straddled me, and I watched him unbutton his shirt. I was shivering as if it was winter time and I thought I was going to throw up on him, but I was too scared he would beat me. He started kissing my neck. I mentally wanted to grabbed his gun. I would have tried to kill him. He crawled on top of me. I begged, "Please! This is not me! You really don't know me. This is not who I am." In my mind, I screamed as loud as I could, "God, save me! Help me, please!"

Instantly, he sat straight up. He glared me in my eyes. "Get your damn stuff and let's go." I complied. The ride was silent.

I busted through Shawnee's door crying, screaming every curse word I could reel off my tongue. Who was anyone to think they could prostitute me out and endanger my life? Katie crying on the couch screaming, "I told them not to do it." I was furious, sick, scared, weak, and wanting to fight. I was dealing with hyenas outnumbered. Katie would be no good. Riha was not there and she was not in the know of the deal. These girls would fight dirty, meaning with knives. Yes, my crew. They kept repeating, "You did not have to do anything," as if he was their only concern. I returned to Shawnee's place in Louisville the following weekend, and the thin man found out I was there. He showed up at Shawnee's place with a completely different look, flowers, and an apology. My crew was dumbfounded by the humbling of this hardcore (unbeknownst to me) drug dealer taking a drastic turn for a girl.

God was my saving grace that night because I was taught and it was embedded in me to call on my Lord and Savior Jesus Christ during any and every circumstance. I will not end this chapter as if the incident magically put me on a straight and narrow path. I spent many years fighting the demons in my mind with beast-like behavior. My question to you is, what demons or beasts are you fighting?

I have learned I serve a great and wonderful God, and He is awesome and loving. God knows the devil will present us with opportunities of destruction, which is why He provides us with a door to exit out. God will not place people in your life who want to harm or derail you or lead you to your destruction. We have an innate device that warns of the danger. It may feel like a tickle or butterflies, or it may be a stranger who says "you don't need to be here." We try to drown out God's and the angels' voices with the pleasures of this world, and God does not desire for us to have a life of misery.

I knew God, and I had to learn to have a personal relationship with Him. Until then, I roamed this earth feeling like a stranger in this land for decades, tormented with a smile and an eternal beast to conqueror. Until then, follow me as I peel away decades of unresolved torment and we work through murder, abuse, molestation, addiction, betrayal, mental illness, grief, or any issue to tame the beast within.

Mother, May I?

STAR WASHINGTON

Mother, may I spend the night at my friend's house? Mother, may I go over to my cousin's house? Mother, may I go to the movies with Uncle Jack and Aunt Susie? As a mom, these are words we hear all too often! It would be ideal if we lived in a world where we could just say, "Of course!" without any precaution. It would be wonderful if the world was a safe haven for our children as it used to be back in our grandparents' days. As a mom of seven, I am highly overprotective of my kids, as my mother was of me. Sometimes no matter how watchful an eye we keep on our babies, danger still finds its way in.

As a parent, it gets harder and harder to know who to trust when it comes to your children. Being a single parent takes a village. You trust that the people in your village love and care for your children as you do, but that isn't always the case. Most predators hide within plain site, and those are the ones who are the most dangerous—the ones who show up at dance recitals, the ones who buy the best gifts at birthday parties, the ones who sit in the stands and cheer your babies on as hard as you do. It becomes hard to tell the real from the fake. My mother worked very hard at giving us the best in life. We went to the best schools. We lived in the best neighborhoods and pretty much had an all-American suburban life. We spent summers with our village, holidays with our village, and spring breaks with our village. When life was throwing her ups and downs and curve balls, it was very important to my mom that we weren't affected, so at one point we went to live with our village.

As I approached the age of 14, I was a frail, skinny thing. I had no shape, no curves—nothing! I made up for it in my outfits. Baby, I could dress my frail butt off. I had moved to spend one school year with my village. I was away from mom and thought I was grown. I was excited for the new school year. I couldn't wait to be the new girl. Y'all know what it's like to be the new girl in high school—all the guys are interested, and you are the hot thing on the block! I was so ready for all of it. My new school was amazing. My village wasn't that strict, so my home life was even better.

One night as I lay asleep, tired from a long day of being the center of attention, I felt a shadowy presence. It was almost like when you watch a scary movie and you can just feel danger right around the corner. I was startled out of my sleep to find someone standing over me masturbating! And it was not just anyone. It was someone I loved. Someone I trusted!

I immediately pretended to fall back asleep, not really knowing how to handle what just happened. The next morning, I stuck it in my mental block and kept moving. Life resumed as normal. I didn't mention it to anyone. I continued with life as if it had never happened. I had a very weird feeling after that but was able to press forward.

Let me remind you all that I thought I was grown, and my village really wasn't that strict, so as any normal teenager does, I did a few things I wasn't supposed to do. I used to love to call my friends back home during my summer visits. Back in the day before cell phones, we had long-distance calling. I ran up a few phone bills calling my friends during the summer. One phone call in particular cost me my soul! I can remember late one evening, I was tucked away in a corner of the home office making yet another long-distance phone call. In walked one of the members of my village. Now, I just knew this was it. I was about to get into a lot of trouble, and life as I knew it was officially over. On the contrary, they mentioned that they knew what I was doing but weren't going to tell and that I could finish my call. Phew! I breathed a huge sigh of relief. I was ecstatic that I not only didn't have to hang up, but wasn't going to get into any trouble either! They came in and sat at the computer as if to do some work as I stayed in my corner having my conversation. Moments later, I looked up to find them sitting in plain sight of me watching porn on the computer and masturbating for me to see. I was completely horrified! I was also frozen in place. I didn't know if I was supposed to get up and leave and just risk getting in trouble for the phone call or if I was supposed to stay put and act like I didn't see it. Luckily, that was a decision I didn't have to make. They finished pleasuring themselves and just casually got up and left the room. I told my friend what had happened and cried to go home.

As the days went by, I played the scene over and over in my mind. I couldn't decide if I should tell someone or not. I could vaguely remember hearing rumors of sexual assault happening to someone I knew closely. I made up in my mind that I was going to tell them. I just didn't know how and when. Taking a shower became awkward, going to sleep became uncomfortable—just being there was becoming a complete problem for me. At night, I could see them walking around the house pleasuring themselves while they thought everyone else was asleep. These are things you do in the confines of your bedroom. These are personal intimate things you just don't do around 14-year-olds. I came home from school one day and decided enough was enough. Today was the day I was going to tell someone. I reached out to someone close who I knew would understand, and they immediately came to my rescue.

Within a few hours, I was packed up and moved to another house, and my mother was on her way. It didn't take long before the news spread throughout the village. Everyone was confused, hurt, and most of all, angry.

Lots of cursing, threats, and fights happened once my mother arrived. It was a very sad scene that tore our village apart. Yes, it takes a village to raise a child, but my village was severely divided. Some believed my stories of what had happened, and others questioned it. There were some who chose to turn a blind eye to what I was saying and that really hurt. I understand that in some cases, people lie about these things, but in my case, I couldn't believe that everyone didn't believe what I was saying. Regardless of the hurt, pain, and anger, not enough was done. There were no real repercussions for the magnitude of what had happened. The village put it in their mental blocks and kept moving forward.

I moved home, finished high school, and moved out on my own. I was an adult doing my own thing. At this point, my life showed no side effects of the trauma I had endured. I was great, life was great, and there was no need to ever mention what had happened. Or so I thought, until the dreadful day my phone rang. When I answered, my worst nightmares were revealed. There was another victim. Oh my gosh, I couldn't believe it. So many years had gone by. Life was normal again. What was going on? How had this happened. Now someone else I loved had to go through my horrible experience on a whole other level. As I listened to her crying in my ear, my heart broke. Her experiences were similar to mine if not worse. What was worse is she wasn't the only other victim. I felt like I had failed her. I had let her down in so many ways. I was ravished with guilt. Should I have done more? Should I have pressed the issue until more was done? She had done exactly what I had—she reached out to who she knew could relate to her story. I was so glad to be her shoulder to cry on, but I hurt for her pain and violation. She didn't deserve this, and neither had I.

One of the biggest mistakes we can make in a sexual abuse case is to take it too lightly. As parents, we can sometimes underestimate the effects it has on our children. In my opinion, no one deserves to be sexually abused in any way. If sexual assault does occur, the perpetrators deserve to be prosecuted. There should not be exceptions just because you know and love the perpetrator. You have to do your part to break the cycle.

It is still a hard subject to discuss. At times, it is taken lightly if there was no sexual intercourse. Molestation doesn't always include sexual intercourse. Unwanted sexual advances, sexual harassment, and unwanted oral sex are all forms of sexual abuse. Just because you weren't actually penetrated doesn't make your sexual abuse any less traumatizing. Being violated in any way can have extreme effects on you as a person.

I am amazed at how overprotective I am as a mother. I thought I had suffered no effects from my ordeal. I was wrong. The simple questions, "Mother, may I go to a friend's house?" "Mother, may I go to the mall?" or "Mother, may I go skating with Uncle Todd and Aunt Marcy?" scare the hell out of me. The fear of allowing my children to be normal children and releasing so much control are the side effects. My children do not have sleepovers at Grandma's too often, and they never have sleepovers at friends' houses. I am always fearful, I always want them close enough to keep a watchful eye. My innocence was stolen and my love taken for granted, and I am forever fearful of it happening to one of my children. The hurt and pain cannot be taken back after it has happened. I am always on my toes trying to prevent it from happening so that I won't have to spend years trying to help them heal. I do not want my babies to have their childhoods taken from them in such a horrific manner.

I am grateful to God for my strength. I am especially thankful for my ability to keep moving forward. Sexual assault can steal your innocence, divide a family, and cause severe after-effects, but it doesn't have to break you. Through prayer, I freed myself from the bondage of hurt, betrayal, and guilt. The devil gets no glory. It all belongs to God. Writing this brought up a lot of suppressed feelings and memories. It took me to places I had not allowed myself to go to mentally or emotionally in years. These memories and feelings have no power over me, because I am free! I no longer consider myself a victim. I am even able to have a healthy and loving relationship with members of my village whom I feel had let me down. I am made free and whole. I won't allow myself to be a victim. I am victorious.

Mother, may I go to the movies? Mother, may I go to a friend's house? Mother, may I spend the night with Grandma and Grandpa?

Yes, of course you can!

No Fairytale Love

SHANIQUA DAVIS

Once upon a time…

Isn't this the way most fairytale stories start off? Well for me, that isn't the case. However, for a very long time, I actually thought I was living my fairytale story. Now that I can sit back and think clearly, I'm not sure why I felt that way, but I'm sure that I'm not the only one. So here goes.

In January of 2006, while attending college, I met Mr. Complicated. Our relationship quickly progressed, and he started coming over to my apartment daily. We became almost inseparable. At the time, I had three other roommates. The roommate closest to me, Nay, had a friend visiting one day while Mr. Complicated was over. The friend immediately noticed Mr. Complicated. Therefore, the next day, she came back over, and she and my roommate told me that he had a girlfriend who went to another school. I took the information and relayed it back to Mr. Complicated, but of course he denied it. By this time, I was so infatuated with him that I took his word for it. Mr. Complicated could have told me the sky was purple and I would have believed it.

As the end of the year 2006 approached and school was on Christmas break, I stayed in town to continue to work my two jobs—one at a law firm and the other at a local jewelry store—while Mr. Complicated returned home. During this time, my little so-called fling began to take a left turn. I called him one day, and a girl answered the phone to tell me that he was unavailable. So, I thought to myself that it must have been his sister or something. I called again the next day, and to my surprise, the same voice answered the phone again and repeated the same thing. Only this time, she ended it with, "This is his girlfriend." My heart was crushed. Although Mr. Complicated and I had not made it official, we were spending a lot of time together, so he was mine. Mr. Complicated also told me on numerous occasions that he loved me. So why in the world would he have a girlfriend? We eventually ended things completely in the next few months, but deep down, I wanted Mr. Complicated.

I entered a new relationship for about two years, and then things began to go sour. Mr. Complicated had kept in touch during that time, so it wasn't very hard for him to ease back into my life. Furthermore, I also prayed for Mr. Complicated and I to get together, only this time I wanted a relationship. And that's exactly what I got.

In September 2009, I moved to Birmingham, and Mr. Complicated and I were finally together. Things immediately started off shaky. I hadn't even been in Birmingham two months when he started making late-night phone calls while in the bathroom, not coming home, and using my car and leaving me at home alone. Fast forward a few months to around January 2010. As Mr. Complicated and I were riding down Lomb Ave, he proceeded to tell me that his baby mother is pregnant. Mr. Complicated already had one child, and he would always speak so negatively about his baby's mother, so I laughed and asked who she was pregnant by. He proceeded to tell me that he was the alleged father. Shocked is the only word to describe my reaction, because I had no words. That was one of the most devastating things I have ever heard. I cried for days. I couldn't eat or sleep, and depression slowly crept in. I began to drink a little more and pop different forms of pills to try and ease the pain of my heart. Guess where Mr. Complicated was? Oh, he was still there, but that did not stop him from continuing to cheat or hang out in the streets. I would go through his phone only to find messages between him and other females, explicit pictures, and so forth. This would cause major arguments that led to physical altercations.

I had become so clever at finding ways to go through Mr. Complicated's phone and preventing him from leaving on the weekends that he had to become clever as well. There were a few times he would offer me alcoholic beverages in hopes that I would fall asleep so he could leave. There was one instance when I noticed something white floating in my drink. He tried to deny having done anything to it and encouraged me to drink it. A few days later, he admitted to putting a Xanax in it so I could fall asleep. The amount of anger I felt and began to harbor took on a whole new level. How could someone who claims to love me drug me without my permission? The anger I harbored steamed from the baby, the cheating, and the verbal and physical abuse. The verbal arguments became more frequent right along with the physical altercations. The physical arguments during this time were something that I felt like I could manage, because we were neck in neck, and he wasn't able to overpower me. So of course, I felt like they weren't "bad enough" for me to leave. But boy was I wrong. Over time, they became worse.

As I just mentioned, I was the queen of searching through Mr. Complicated's phone and his social media. Mr. Complicated hated the fact that I always found a way to search through his things. He would call me "stupid," "dumb little girl," and "retarded" and always find a way to reverse the situation and make me out to be the one in the wrong. He had become so great at using his words to verbally assault me that I lost all self-esteem and felt guilty for things that I shouldn't have. I began to abandon my family and friends, and I didn't want to go anywhere for fear of an altercation. You see, Mr. Complicated didn't have a car for a while, so any time I wanted to go anywhere, there was always a problem, because it would prevent him from hanging out.

No one knew about the things I was experiencing except for my good friend Vic. There was one instance where Mr. Complicated and I got into an altercation and he choked me, burned my birth control, and took my car and phone. I can remember hyperventilating on my apartment balcony because I was so angry. I walked to the gas station that was nearby to call Vic and asked Vic to come get me. She came, of course, and asked me what was wrong, but I couldn't tell her in the moment due to embarrassment. Vic was always the person I would call when I needed help. She would do her best to be my voice of reason, but there was no voice of reason because I knew that I had prayed for Mr. Complicated, and that's exactly what I got.

Fast forward to 2011. Mr. Complicated and I were still together and still fighting. Things had not improved, but I was still hoping for the best. We moved into one of his family members' houses and things progressively became worse. Yet I still wasn't ready to leave. The verbal abuse had become so frequent, and he would now do it in front of people. One night, Mr. Complicated and I went out with another couple, Kim and Robert. Mr. Complicated and I got into an argument, and as we were pulling into the driveway of the house, he began to call me "stupid," "dumb bitch," and so forth. Embarrassed and not having the energy to respond, I froze. I could not gather up one word to respond to him in hopes that we would not get to fighting in front of Kim and Robert. He repeatedly called me "bitch" to the point where Kim spoke up. However, it didn't stop him. He laughed and continued while Robert tried to convince Kim to stay out of it. Later that night, Mr. Complicated forced himself on top of me. I tried to fight him off, but to no avail. Sex was one of the many tactics Mr. Complicated would use to control and manipulate our situation, often nonconsensually. Torn between the "I love you"s, "Nobody wants you but me"s, name calling, nonconsensual sex, and physical abuse, I still hadn't had enough. Now don't get me wrong, I was fighting back, but it was so out of my character. I had become so mentally and physically drained that I questioned everything about myself. I wondered why I wasn't good enough for this man for whom I had prayed. I knew that I needed to leave, but Mr. Complicated always had a way of reeling me back in.

The physical fights became more prevalent, and each gradually became harsher. Again, Mr. Complicated had not been able to overpower me just yet, but I had become so tired of fighting fair that I started to use objects. I would throw anything that was in reach when a physical fight commenced—lamps, coffee tables, books, two-by-four boards. I knew that one of us had to leave or one of us was going to get seriously hurt.

While on a family vacation, I mistakenly answered my phone, as Mr. Complicated was calling. My cousin and I were passing a sex store and talking about different sex toys. Mr. Complicated swore up and down that he heard men talking and accused me of cheating. Again, I was every name that could be thought of—"bitch," "slut," "whore," and so forth. By the time I returned home, Mr. Complicated packed my clothes in black bags and had them waiting by the door. I immediately grabbed them and begin walking to the car with them. Nevertheless, he had different plans. He attempted to stop me from placing the bags in the car, and as a result, a fight ensued. We wrestled, and Mr. Complicated was able to throw me to the ground and hold me there for a moment while I struggled to get up. I cried and wrestled with him until I had no more energy left. He grabbed the couple of bags that I made it to the car with and put them back in the house. The following day, I woke up, and my intuition told me to log into his PlayStation and check his videos. As I was doing so, I ran across a video of him having sex with the girl who answered the phone when we were in college and said that she was his girlfriend. She had indeed been his girlfriend during that time. From the time I moved to Birmingham, she had basically never left the picture. I would often see text messages and phone calls between the two of them, so seeing them together wasn't much of a surprise. However, I was surprised to see that Mr. Complicated had chosen to have sex with her in the home where we lived together.

Okay, so I finally decided that enough was enough. My clothes were still packed, so I left and went to live with Vic for a few weeks until I found an apartment. Mr. Complicated called for a few weeks to try and get me to come back, but I was standing strong. Well, at least for a few weeks. Once again, I let Mr. Complicated ease back in my life. The year 2012 crept in, and Mr. Complicated moved into my new apartment. Again, he wasn't working and had no car. Only this time, he couldn't use my car as frequently, because I used it for work. Nevertheless, Mr. Complicated was still up to his same tricks—cheating, verbal and physical abuse, hanging out late, and taking my car. Every time we got into an argument this time around, he would grab the neck of whatever shirt I had on and rip it. Therefore, in addition to all the altercations, I was also having to purchase new shirts often.

Overall, I had become completely drained and empty inside, but I stayed. I stayed because I was broken. Over the course of 2012, Mr. Complicated and I had been in multiple altercations, one in which I called the police. He had taken my car and not returned it, broken my apartment window on two different occasions, broken two flat-screen TVs, and ruined large amounts of my clothing. Yet, I stayed. I knew that this relationship was toxic, but I couldn't break that tie.

Vic had a habit of texting me pictures of her outfits as she was trying them on, so I could give her my opinion. As I was sitting on the couch one day going through the pictures she was sending, Mr. Complicated snatched my phone out of my hand and said, "Bitch, gimme that phone. I knew your ass was gay." He then proceeded to punch me in the top of my head with so much strength that I blacked out for a second. I jumped up, stumbling, trying to gain my composure, thinking that I was about to fight back, only to look him in his eyes and see something that I've never seen before. This wasn't going to be one of those regular fights where I could handle myself. Fear overcame my body, and I remember thinking in that moment that I was going to lose my life. Gasping for air while Mr. Complicated was choking me, I knew I had to fight and get away. My head was pounding, and I could hear his children screaming and crying as they witnessed us fighting. I wrestled myself away and made my way to the door when he caught me by the shirt and ripped my clothes off, down to my underwear. I was screaming, the kids were screaming, and he was yelling, calling me a bitch and a whore. Kicking myself away from him, I headed to the door again and made it outside in just my underwear. I screamed and yelled, "Help! Help me!" as loudly as a could, hoping that someone would hear me and come to the rescue. I made it about twenty feet away from the door before Mr. Complicated caught up and grabbed me from behind, covering my mouth. He pulled me back in the house with his arm around my neck from the back and his hand covering my mouth. Unable to put up much of a fight, I remember being too scared to put up a fight anyway. I think the only thing that saved my life that night was the area in which I lived. It was a predominately white apartment complex in Hoover, and the city was known for having a small tolerance policy. They didn't mind taking people to jail, and I think Mr. Complicated thought about that because he wasn't sure if my neighbors had called the police or not. It took me almost losing my life to realize that I had to end this, and I had to end this quickly.

Yet again, it still wasn't quite the ending. I continued to have sex with Mr. Complicated from time to time, only this time I was more cautious. I didn't let him know where I lived, and I would only go to his house. I picked him up one day to take him to run some errands, and we got into an argument. Nothing had changed. Mr. Complicated was still verbally abusive, and I was still all types of bitches and whores. I met someone else in 2013. I dated him for almost three years, and I left Mr. Complicated alone during that time. However, that relationship ended, and Mr. Complicated once again eased back into my life.

Things started off a little differently this time, but there were still red flags and dishonesty. It was still a problem if I wanted to hang out with friends or family. I was called a "slut" once for studying with male classmates. He said it with so much passion and force behind his voice that I once again became speechless. I knew at that moment that we could never be, yet still that soul tie was so strong that it wasn't enough to stop me from hanging with Mr. Complicated from time to time. It wasn't until the middle of 2017 that the sex became unfulfilling. I was in the middle of having sex with Mr. Complicated and determined in that moment that I was done and had to move on. I knew that I had achieved something great when I was able to no longer answer his phone calls or see him and be able to say "no" and continue my day.

Soul ties are real. The soul tie I had lasted for over 10 years. I would pray for that tie be broken only to continue to walk right back into it due to fear of moving on and allowing someone else to do the same thing. For years, I felt alone, embarrassed, and scared. It wasn't until I begin to talk about it that I was able to move on and not think twice about going back. Also, I realized that I wasn't alone. Many women experience similar situations but are also too afraid to discuss it. I had to continuously pray for strength and understand that just because someone tells you they love you or vice versa doesn't mean that you are meant to be. Find someone who loves you unconditionally and makes you question everything that you ever thought was love in the past. I did. Love doesn't hurt!

He Loves Me, He Loves Me Not

MELISSA MOREHEAD

"The hunger for love is much more difficult to remove than the hunger for bread."
—Mother Teresa

We have all heard the words, "Why did you stay?" "I would have never stayed in that situation," "He is not all that," and "If that is his way of showing her love, I would hate to see his hatred towards her." These were the same words that I would say all the time when I would see a woman on a talk show talking about staying in an abusive relationship. These were not the words I thought I would hear from people. It seems like yesterday that the same words came for me when the first blow came to my face. I recalled the conversation that I would have with myself about these women. You see, I now became that woman. I was that woman. The woman who went from standing for nothing to falling for anything. I was confused as to why this was happening to me.

I was not raised in this environment, nor did I want my children to be in this environment.

Let me back up to move forward. I was raised in a loving, two-parent home. My father was a hard-working man who loved the Lord, provided for his wife and family, and doted on his girls. My mother was a stay-at-home mother (later returning to work when my sister and I entered into middle school and high school, respectively), and who also exemplified to her daughters the true meaning of a godly woman. There were many kids with whom to play in our neighborhood growing up. For the most part, we all got along well, playing favorite childhood games, including Ring around the Rosie; Duck, Duck, Goose; and Mother, May I? to name a few. There were times when I did not want to interact with the other kids. When I got into this mood, you could find me with a flower playing my favorite game—He Loves Me, He Loves Me Not. I would always make sure that I would end up on "he loves me." Something about pulling that last rose petal gave me butterflies in my stomach, and I truly believed that is what love felt like—the anticipation, the excitement, the overwhelming feeling of joy.

Unfortunately, when I became an adult and involved with the opposite sex, I figuratively let this game be the foundation of my relationships. I based love on a rose petal instead of on the Word of God, which states that, "love is patient, love is kind. It does not envy, it does not boast, it is not proud. It does not dishonor others, it is not self-seeking, it is not easily angered, it keeps no records of wrongs. Love does not delight in evil but rejoices in the truth. It always protects, always trust, always hopes, always preserves. Love never fails" (1 Corinthians 13:4-8).

You see, I was a young girl when I gave birth to a baby girl. At this time in my life, I was making decisions based on my desires, and guess what? Those desires cost me greatly! I met a young man who eventually would become the father of my two sons. We married young, not having a clue about being married, being parents, paying bills, and all of the responsibilities that go along with being a married couple. By the time I was 23 years old, I had three children and was very unhappy in a marriage that made me confused with myself. I asked myself, "Why did I get married? Why am I still here? What am I doing wrong to deserve this kind of treatment? Does he really and truly love me?" The basis of my love or feeling of love went back to the last rose petal that I remember pulling as a young girl.

Unbeknownst to me, at six months pregnant, it all started with the one question that I politely asked—"Can you help me?" Had I known that a simple question would have put him in a wrath of anger, I would not have asked. After he did not answer, I asked him again, "Can you help me put the groceries away?" I clearly remember like it was yesterday. He was sitting in the recliner holding our one-year-old son. He calmly got out of the recliner, placing our son on the floor, came into the kitchen, and smacked me across my face. I was shocked, shaken, and sore. The hit was powerful and sweaty. He dared me to fight back; I took that dare as a threat and threw a bag of frozen peas at his back. Why did I do this? This angered him. He hurled at me with fire in his eyes, hatred in his voice, and evilness in his touch. You might recall that I stated that I was pregnant. Yes, big and pregnant.

My protruding belly did not get in his way, my screams did not stop him, and my young, helpless son crying at the top of his lungs did not bring him to his senses. I do believe that the noise increased his adrenaline to go stronger and harder. This was just the beginning of what was to come. This had become a way of life that to which I was not accustomed; this all took me by surprise, as he did not display any signs of being an abuser while we were dating.

Despite the boundaries that I had set, along with the environment in which I was living, I still loved him and just knew he loved me. After all, he apologized after every attack, held me, and even bought me items that he just knew I would love. You might say that this is silly, absurd, and totally irresponsible. You have to realize that at that point in my life, it was a control issue for him and a self-esteem issue for me. Throughout our time together, the abuse intensified. A smack gradually turned into a punch, a hit gradually turned into a blow, and a blow to the head gradually went to the unthinkable injuries.

The physical abuse was eventually accompanied by mental abuse as well. He called me names and told me that I was ugly and no one would ever want me. The sad part is that I started to believe in what he said. (I now realize that was a lie, and I was being deceived by what he saw in me.) After our altercations, he would go buy me gifts ranging from roses, to clothing, and to a computer. After our physical encounters, he would want to engage in intimacy, regardless of how I felt physically, mentally, and emotionally. When this occurred, I felt desperate, dirty, and devastated. Without fail, I would vomit immediately. The vomiting made me feel better, like I was purging all of the emotions.

This situation started affecting my children. People would constantly ask me why I stayed. I felt as if I had to lie and make up excuses for his behavior. I would respond and say I was scared of his next attack, as I had previously stated that the abuse was much stronger and harder each time. To be truthful, I stayed as an obligation to my children and to the mounting debt. I also did not want to become another statistic. However, I did not realize staying made me a statistic.

Eventually, there came a turning point in this situation. The night before, we had a bad argument, which led into a bad fight. My neighbors ended up intervening, and he finally left the house that night. After this particular fight, I had had enough of the abuse and all of his shenanigans. I told him, "Tonight, someone is leaving with a tag on their toe, and guess what? It is not going to be me."

The next day, I woke up and started my day making a determination that this was the day I was going to file charges and a restraining order against him. Although the kids were at daycare, I took them with me in my heart and in my mind. I was doing this for them, for us, and for myself. I figured upon arrival that I would be in and out in no time with what I needed to start my life over the right way.

Unfortunately, things didn't go as planned. The gentleman assigned to my case clearly told me over and over again that if I pressed charges, I would not receive child support, as he would be unemployed and not be able to seek employment. I could not believe what I was hearing. Was he on my husband's side? Clearly he misunderstood my reason for being there today. I believed he was under the impression that I was not going to follow through with the process.

Repeatedly, I assured him that I was not having second thoughts of not wanting to file. I would go through with this legal matter. He assured me that he understood my pain. I wondered, if he really did understand my pain, then why would he tell me again, "If you press charges, you will not receive child support. You are currently pregnant. How will you feed your kids with only one income? How will you pay for daycare expenses with one income?" I politely grabbed my belongings and thanked the gentleman for his time and partial assistance. I cannot begin to tell you what kind of emotions ran through me. Although I worked in the legal field, at this particular time, my belief in the justice system was immediately fading away.

Once I entered my vehicle, I felt defeated and violated and was starting to wonder if this is what the saying, "This is a man's world" meant. If so, it was a wrap for me, and I was a done deal. At this time, we were still married but now living separately. I decided to take the children and leave him. I no longer wished to expose them to this environment of negativity, self-doubt, and abuse. As a mother, I was willing to protect my children at all cost, even if it meant leaving him for good. I had to make up my mind. No more reconciliation.

I left a nice townhouse in a quiet, and safe environment and moved to an area where the crime rate was off the charts. The roaches were extended family and the rodents made themselves at home wherever they felt welcome. Not a night passed without hearing gunshots, arguments, or drunk residents and their guests outside of the window. I felt that I had hit rock bottom and had no other choice but to turn to God. I cried and prayed to God to help me through this matter.

I said, "Dear God, protect my children from the violence that I have exposed them to. Give me the strength to leave this situation alive and quickly. Help me and my children leave safely and peacefully. Lord, in the process, please make me a better and stronger mother. In Jesus's name, I pray. Amen." During this time in my life, my belief in God was strong, but my faith lacked. I knew who He was, but I did not understand fully who He was. I would recall reading the scriptures in Isaiah 54:17: "No weapon formed against me will prosper."

However, if God stated that no weapon will not form, why was this abuse happening to me? What was I to do? I paid more attention to the "weapon" than the promise that it would not prosper. It was not until I received a job transfer to Seattle, Washington, after my cry for help and my pleas and prayers to God that I finally understood how He operates and how He was operating. I noticed He operates in his time and on His schedule, but it was a suddenly moment. "Suddenly" in the Webster's Dictionary is defined as "quickly and unexpectedly." Suddenly, we were moving across the country, to another state and another time zone. I was excited. However, the suddenly was overshadowed by my finding out that my children could not accompany me for several months. What was I to do in that time? I could not leave the kids in his care or in the environment where he was currently living. I had to think fast, and I do mean fast. I was devastated, torn, and heartbroken.

What was I to do? We were still married and both had equal rights to the kids. I was not going to give up without a fight. He had already threatened to take the kids from me, stating that "I would never see them again." As a mother, it was my duty to defend them and protect them at all costs. He was informed of the move and immediately stated that he would come by the day prior to our departure to spend time with the kids. Little did he know, the kids were not leaving just yet. I devised a plan for the children to stay with my godparents in the same city and state until I was able to reunite with them. While I was gone, the kids were living 30 minutes away from him. I prayed every night that he would not find out and go get them.

For months, he would call to speak to them. I would respond that they were either asleep or did not want to talk. I was starting to run out of excuses, and he was starting to become suspicious of my excuses. Although he did not say it, I am sure he wanted to know why they are always sleeping or never wanted to talk to him. I went into mommy mode. I had to now pick up my children from their godparents' and bring them back with my family living in Indiana. My parents drove twelve hours nonstop to retrieve my kids. A late evening arrival to retrieve my kids was purposely planned. All of this took place within 48 hours. My children were safe and away from my now ex-husband. They were now in a safe haven built on trust, laughter, peace, love, togetherness, and God. The move left an unresolved issue of not knowing the next time he would see them and when they would have interaction with him.

For the next five years, we tried communicating peacefully about issues with the children, ranging from education, to religion, to extracurricular activities, to disciple. It never failed that our conversations ended up with us arguing and him constantly reminding me that I was not anything and would never become anything in life. Who would ever want me with three kids?

Fast forward to years later. My employment obligation had expired, and I moved back to my hometown of Indiana with my children. Recovering from the divorce and memories of the abuse was not easy. He and I finally moved past the bad attitudes, cursing sessions, and the thought of wanting to get revenge on everything when we came in contact. I had to keep reminding myself not to take revenge, but to leave room for God's wrath, for it is written: "'It is mine to avenge, I will repay,' says the Lord" (Romans 12:19). Time had expired between us. He only saw his children twice after we moved back to Indiana.

The only thing I did to free myself was forgive him for what he did to me, to us, and to our family. We have to remember that forgiveness is not for the one who did the act, but more for yourself to let go, to move on, to grow, and to build on your future. He has since passed away, and I am grateful to God that I forgave him prior to his untimely and unexpected death. After his death, I struggled with trust in relationships. I also struggled with a man raising his voice at me I would become defensive and immediately think he was out to get me. It has been through prayer, reading his Word, and fasting that I have been able to overcome always being the victim. I purposely remind myself that I am more than what I have been through.

Ladies, hear me and hear me well. Although love is an action, it is not hitting. Although love is a sound, it is not screaming. Although love is a feeling, it is not fear. No longer should you allow your past to dictate your future. Look into your future with clarity, knowing that you have a Savior who gives you strength. Look into your future without turning back or away from your adversities, as I am reminded in James 1:2 that we are to consider it pure joy, my brothers and sisters, whenever you face trials of many kinds.

Most importantly, always remember to love yourself first. While writing this chapter, I had a breakthrough with myself. I forgave myself for thinking that it was me who caused the drama and the issues with the relationship and our marriage. Self-love is the best love and best medicine that one can have and give. Live your life to the fullest. As William W. Purkey said, "You've got to dance like no one is watching, love like you have never been hurt, sing like there's nobody listening, and live like it's heaven on earth."

Face the Facts

JAMIE OLIVER

Hebrews 11:1 reads, "Now faith is the substance of things hoped for, the evidence of things not seen." At an early age, my faith kicked in. I confessed Christ and was baptized at Oak Grove Missionary Baptist in Brighton, Alabama at the age of eight. Through sermons, I had been taught to believe that Jesus was the Son of God, that He rose from the dead with all power in His hands, and that I was saved by grace. I was a little girl at this time and didn't pay much attention to the sermons. It wasn't until I started attending Sunday School and Vacation Bible School that I began to understand more about who God was to me and that I desired a deeper relationship with Him. I remember seeing people walk to the altar and shake the pastor's hand to join the church, and they later were baptized. One day, I asked my mom, "Ma, can I get baptized?" She said, "Yes!" and asked me if I believed. Never did I imagine that after confessing Christ and getting baptized I would be faced with so many challenges in the years to come.

In the summer of 1990, my family and I had moved from a small house on Smith Street in

Brighton, Alabama to a bigger house on Main Street. I lived with my mom, stepfather, sister, and brother. This was the prime time of our life, because my mom and stepfather were doing an excellent job as parents working and trying to provide for our household. I had just transferred to a better school, Midfield Elementary, and I was a happy, thriving little girl. Little did I know, my family was about to face a tragic loss.

The next year, on July 27, 1991, I had spent the night at my father's house and was awaken by the most horrible news a child could hear. My 17-year-old brother died in a car accident. I had other siblings, however, my brother was my protector. I really looked up to him. He was one of the humblest people you could ever meet and was fine as wine (milk chocolate brown). He looked out for me and made sure I was taken care of. The death of my brother was a turning point in my life. I was nine years old when he passed, and I didn't know much about death. All I knew was that I would never see my brother again. I began to feel a void in my life, and many days I would find myself in a zone trying to figure out why he had to die.

Many years passed. I began to grow up, and puberty started. During this time, my mom and stepfather worked at a local hospital, formerly known as Bessemer Carraway Hospital, where they worked long and countless hours. My mom was a janitor in Environmental Services, and my stepfather was a supervisor. They had recently opened a cleaning service where they cleaned clinics and doctors' offices for extra money. I was now the only child at home, because my sister moved out, which meant I had too much time on my hands and was all alone. I was under minimal supervision unless I was at a family member or friend's house. I hated going to visit other people sometimes because all there was to do was sit for hours and wait on my parents.

My biological father was in my life, and he was a great father. He always made sure he took care of his girls, no matter what he had to do. However, my father was an alcoholic, which limited the time he and I were able to spend together. This was a major issue for me. I would visit him when I wasn't with my aunts or grandmother. I can remember feeling so lonely on the inside. I didn't quite understand why my mom and stepdad worked so much. Because of the loneliness, I made myself comfortable by eating unhealthy food. Growing up, I was a skinny, light-skinned girl with light brown eyes. Eating unhealthy foods and not exercising caused me to gain a lot of weight, so much so that I became self-conscious about myself. I went from a skinny little girl to a chunky pre-teen, which led me to having low self-esteem.

At this time of my life, I didn't like the person I had become. Around the age of 12, I was approached by a young man. We were at the Blue Store, which was a corner store down the street from my aunt's house. The young man gave me his phone number on a brown paper sack and asked me to call him. I was so nervous I lost his number. I couldn't believe I was being approached by him. For years, I watched my friends date boys, but I did not. I didn't go many places outside of family members' and friends' houses, so I didn't have much of a social life. In my mind, I didn't think I was pretty enough to have a boyfriend. I didn't have the big breasts and booties like some of my friends did. As a matter of fact, my mom worked so much that sometimes I didn't even have my hair combed. My mom and aunt put a jerry curl in my hair for a little while, and once, my mom gave me a press and curl. Now you know, I hated that press and curl! I would have rather looked like a chicken than get my hair combed. My sister moved back home for a little while and was getting her hair done at the shop. I was able to convince my mom to allow me to go with her. Getting my hair done gave me more confidence in myself, and my self-esteem began to increase. I began to like myself a little more. The summer leading up to my ninth grade, I started exercising and eating less so that I could start to feel better about myself.

Fast forward to one year later. I was sitting on my grandmother's porch with my aunt, and behold, that same guy who approached me before was with one of my cousins walking down the street and stopped by my grandmother's house. I wanted to run in the house so fast. I almost started having a panic attack. He approached me, and we all began to talk and laugh. Before leaving, he told me his name was William, and we exchanged numbers. We began to talk on the phone, and he would come visit me. He was a cool guy, so we connected right away. Now, I knew I hadn't discussed dating with my mom, and I knew it would possibly be an issue, so I would go down my grandmother and aunts' houses so I could see him. I was only 13 when William and I began dating. William was this short little thang too, which made it easy for me to hide the fact that he was five years older than me. He was cute and dark chocolate brown, like I like.

William and I began to develop a friendship, and he stepped in and filled the void that was in my heart from the death of my brother, my father being a drunk, being bullied by the kids calling my dad a wino, and my parents working so much.

Having my older boyfriend made me feel secure, built my self-esteem, and made me feel accomplished and in the in crowd of my peers, so I thought. We had a lot in common. We both were broken. He was broken due to growing up without a father in his home. He was a great boyfriend in the beginning. He used to buy me anything I wanted, and he did things that I wanted to do. We went to sporting events, the park, and the movies, and many times, we visited my family. A lot of my family liked him.

Later that year, I met this girl who lived down the street from me. We became friends, and during a visit, she warned me that William was abusive to a previous girlfriend. I was so caught up in William that I believed I was the exception until I got a reality check about a year later. William was in the streets doing things with which I did not agree, including cheating with other females and other things that I believed was detrimental to both our lives. At this point, in my mind, I had had enough, and I had started to find interest in other boys at my school. William and I had started to get into aggressive arguments, and I knew it was time to leave the situation.

The day I broke up with him, he was angry, but he asked to come over, and I allowed him to. I should have never said yes. I knew better than to have company over while my parents were at work. I should have used that as my excuse, but I didn't. I didn't know that night would be the beginning of many years of abuse. We had heated discussions before, but I had been able to walk away. This time was not like before. Before I could walk away, he jumped up off the bed and grabbed the oil sheen bottle, hit me upside my head with it, and pushed my head into the wall. I was screaming and crying for my life. This attack left me with a bruised and swollen eye and a knot on my head. My sister called the police, and this is when my family found out he was five years older than me. Oh, did I mention that William and I had been having sex for over a year now? I begged my mother not to press charges against him. I could remember just praying to God, because I really didn't understand what I was in.

Months later, after I had become lonely again and he continued to ask me back into his life, I gave in. This time, he promised never to hit me again. I can remember him threatening me if I didn't take him back. There was still verbal abuse sometimes before this incident, but I could handle that—just not the physical. Just as it is the case with most couples, disagreements arose. He always called me a nerd because he said I was so smart. William would make fun of my glasses and my little breasts. He would call my breasts ant bites. Now looking back, I realize that these were all signs of emotional and mental abuse. He was saying these things to me to tear down who I was as a person and make me feel bad about myself. Nevertheless, I would try to encourage him because I was in love with him, and I thought in my mind that he was this way because he didn't have a high school diploma and he wasn't happy about his dad not being in his life. I loved him for who he was as a person and the good I saw in him, and I wanted him to be happy. So much so that we planned to have a child together.

I was on the depo shot, and it was causing me health issues, so I switched to the pill. Well that wasn't a good idea, and I knew I would probably forget, so this was my excuse to get pregnant.

In March of 1998, I missed my cycle, and I was feeling a little sick. I figured I was pregnant, so I scheduled an appointment at Save A Life in Bessemer, Alabama. At my appointment, they confirmed that I was pregnant and gave me my options. I had no doubt in my mind. I knew I was going to keep this baby. I was so afraid to tell my mom, but I was still excited. About a week later, I started to spot as if I was starting my menstrual period. I was praying, "Lord, please don't let me lose the baby." Unfortunately, I had a miscarriage. We were so devastated. William and I grieved.

In the back of my mind, I wanted a child to love. I can remember when I got pregnant for the second time. Toward the end of May of 1998, William, my family, and I got a hotel room and went swimming. Weeks later, I went a local clinic, and they confirmed that I was pregnant. Three months into my pregnancy, we were attending the African American Heritage Festival, and I ordered a virgin daiquiri. The acid from the drink started to make me nauseous. I began to throw up and was ready to go, but William got upset and asked, "Why do you keep throwing up?" I knew I was spoiling his fun, but I couldn't help it. Hell, I was the one pregnant. He was mad and acting like he was tired of me being sick. If you know me and my attitude, I got frustrated. I said, "If I knew you were going to treat me this way, I would've gotten an abortion." Well, what did I say that for? He was like, "Let's go!" We began to walk to the parking deck to leave. To my surprise, he grabbed a tall plastic container out my hand and started to beat me with it. I ran and got in the car, and he grabbed me by my ponytail while I was sitting in the car and continued to hit me. He kept hitting me, and I was very afraid for my life. Now, here we were again in a domestic dispute. I was pregnant now. What was I going to do with a baby and no baby daddy? I don't even remember if I went to the hospital to get checked or not. I just remember praying to God that nothing was wrong with my baby. Because of the love I had for William, I started apologizing and blaming myself. The next episode was when I was seven months pregnant. I knew William was still cheating, but I stayed with him. I began to focus on my pregnancy. He and I were driving down the highway, and his beeper was going off. I commented about it, and he lost it. He hit me so hard in my face and kept hitting me trying to make me wreck. I was so afraid for my baby, and I begged him to stop. When I got to his grandmother's house, I had to beg him to get out the car. I felt worthless. How could someone do this to a woman they say they love and furthermore is carrying their son. I lied and told him that I wasn't gonna tell anyone, but I went straight home and told my mom that I needed to go to the hospital to check the baby. I asked my mom to promise not to tell them exactly what had happened. On February 24, 1999, I had my first son at 8:58 a.m. after 15 hours of dry labor. He weighed seven pounds, 11.4 ounces and was 19 inches long.

Going through these challenges grew my faith in God. There were many days I wanted to give up. I even gave up on church because I felt ashamed and embarrassed. I felt like no one at church would accept the fact that I had a child out of wedlock, let alone that my baby daddy wasn't the ideal boyfriend and protector for my son. I found myself praying and talking to God because I knew He was the only one who would understand. Even through the abuse, we stayed together, had two more children, and got married. One day in June of 2007, enough was enough. My enough came with a knife to my neck with my nine-month-old baby girl in my arms.

I knew that I wasn't perfect either. I also knew how to push William and make him upset. I will not put all the blame on him, but one thing I can say is I didn't disrespect him and put my hands on him in a violent way unless I felt threatened by his actions. To this day, I blame myself for staying in this abusive relationship because it has affected my entire family. If you are reading this chapter, I want you to know that there is a better way and that we have choices. I know it is desirable to have the older, hip boyfriend who all the girls are hovering over, but if he is abusive and doesn't respect you, then make a conscious decision to leave the situation, because the abuse can have a major impact on your life and possibly can end in death or you being damaged for the rest of your life.

You see, I know my real truth will not help everyone who reads this book, but my objective is to be able to help at least one young girl or woman who may be experiencing these issues that I experienced. If you are experiencing a loss or a void in your life, be careful of the decisions you make. Do not try to fill a void with a man or tangible things. Only God can give you the peace and comfort that you are seeking. It took much prayer and supplication and many nights of crying out to God for me to walk away from the mental, physical, and emotional abuse. Jeremiah 29:11 reads, "'For I know the thoughts that I think of you,' saith the Lord. 'Thoughts of peace, and not of evil, to give you an expected end.'" If you are experiencing abuse, turn to God, get into a Bible-based church, and/or surround yourself with people who truly love you. It took me years to realize that love doesn't hurt. You don't have to make the same mistakes I did. God gave us free choice and allows us to make our own decisions. You deserve to be loved, not abused.

Did You Really Know?

VICTORIA NECOLE

Most little girls are taught that they shouldn't have sex until they are married and that if they had a positive male figure in their life, they would want to marry someone like him. But what happens to the little girls who don't get a chance at a "normal life"? What happens to the little girls who have their innocence robbed at a young age? What happens to the little girls who are abandoned by their fathers?

What about the little girls who are fondled with, molested, and/or raped as child? What about the girls who were never told that they should wait, that they are more than a sex object? What about the little girls who were told "as long as you have what's between your legs you should never go without," and because they didn't have positive role models, they didn't understand that this was a joke and took those very words and ran with them? Do they stand a chance of living a happily ever after life like the ones in all the children's book they'll read growing up?

Well, this was me. My mother and father divorced when I was five years old, and I didn't get a chance to officially meet him until I was 15 when

I decided to move to Atlanta to live with him my junior year of high school. He wasn't ready to be a father. He was an alcoholic, and on my first night, he shook the bed I was lying in because he couldn't catch his balance to get up and go to the bathroom. Atlanta is where I had my first "real" homosexual experience with a "mature" girl. I was also almost raped at the age of 15. Shortly after that incident, my mother came and took me back home, and I wasn't allowed to visit my dad again until I was 18. My dad didn't show back up again until I was graduating from high school. He popped up here and there, but he wasn't physically present. Even on my graduation day, he made it all about himself. He was seen driving in a drop-top convertible that he rented with the graduation money he had promised me.

When I was growing up, my mother's relationships didn't display what a happy home should be like. There were always fights and arguments. Dishes and china were being thrown around the house, and I couldn't tell you how many cordless phones we went through during my adolescent years. The only man that I did like was involved in other activities, and his relationship with my mom didn't last but a couple of years. When they broke up, I was devastated. I secretly blamed my mother for not trying hard enough to make their relationship work. He was the first man who made me feel safe. When he looked at me, I never felt that he wanted anything from me sexually (the way other men made me feel).

At the age of seven, I was molested by a female relative. I remember it as if it happened yesterday. We sat on my grandmother's brown, smoke-infested couch that slightly slumped to the left and placed next to the floor model television. I stared at her attentively as she told me what to do. "Climb up on me and place your hand right here," she said as she pointed toward her breast.

I guess she felt my hesitation or saw the fear in my eyes, because she replied, "If you do what I tell you, I will let you have the leftover waffles that are in the refrigerator." Although I wasn't hungry and her proposition gave me no comfort, I couldn't say no to her. I remember looking at how sad she looked. I told myself, "Just do it. It will all be over soon." After, all I was raised to obey adults without question. I felt stuck between a rock and a hard place, so I just did it. I did exactly what she instructed me to do.

I climbed on top of her and took her fully grown breast into my mouth, kissing and licking it all while she was rubbing on me. The thought of this is disgusting, but she moaned. I had no idea what that meant, so I continued kissing and licking until she told me to stop. "This is our little secret, and no one can know," she said to me. "No one would believe you anyway. Now go to the fridge and get the waffles." I stood there with the door open and stared at the Styrofoam container. I wasn't hungry earlier, and I wasn't hungry now. Not wanting to disappoint her, I reached in the drawer, grabbed a fork, and proceeded to break off a piece of waffle and place it in my mouth. It was wet and soggy, so much so that I became sick to my stomach and couldn't finish. I put it in the trash and hid it in the plastic bag. I kept my secret from my family until I was 31 years old. I felt as if the incident was my fault—that I should have known better, that I somehow, I asked for it to happen. I later found out that she had been molested.

From that moment with her, my sexual activity began to rise. I thought her behavior with me was normal. I thought playing house or doctor with other little girls was okay. The other little girls in the neighborhood would touch and kiss each other sometimes, so who was I to think differently? By the age of 10, I had been fondled with by five other little girls, and I liked it. I didn't lose my virginity to a male until I was 17, but even on that day, a girl whom I would allow to perform oral sex was in the same room. I remember that day vividly. Once we got to his apartment, we all watched TV. Neisha was that "down for whatever" friend. She "jumped off the porch" way before I did. Girls, guys, whatever, it didn't matter. She was down for whatever with whoever, whenever. And if you are wondering, yes, she and I had been together sexually as well.

Looking back, I can't remember when she and I started hanging out or when I got so comfortable with her that I never asked her to leave the room. This night, Philly and I were lying in his bed when we started making out. We were heavy on making out and touching, but tonight was different. I had decided this was going to be it. I wanted to go all the way. It wasn't painful, and I didn't cry, but it wasn't magical either. There were no rainbows, gumdrops, or lollipops, and to my surprise, no blood.

As I began to gather myself together, Neisha followed me into the bathroom.

"You okay girl?" she asked. I had told her earlier that tonight was the night.

"Yeah, I'm good." I didn't give her many details.

Now, this isn't making any sense to you, I know. Like many of you, I didn't think being fingered or having someone perform oral sex on me was considered sex if I didn't repeat the act or it wasn't between me and a male. Boy, was I wrong. Per research, any sexual contact is considered sex, no matter if it is oral, anal or vaginal. But like many of you, I didn't realize I had lost my virginity at the age of seven.

I went from being sexually abused to sexually abusing myself. After having sex for the first time, I became addicted to the way it felt. During my sexual encounters, I felt love. I felt wanted. I felt in control. In less than four months after having sex for the first time, I had sex with five other men—men who I had just met and men whom I had known for some time but didn't want them to be my "first."

After graduating high school and moving to Alabama, I felt that I could start my life over and no one would know about my sex addiction, but that was far from truth. My first semester of college started off normally. I was dating someone, and we both decided that sex was not a topic of discussion. We respected each other enough to wait until we got married. However, not talking about sex did not last long. I thought this was my chance to start over. I told him about my past, he accepted it, and we never talked about it again. The next semester, he moved back to his hometown, I was left alone again, and my desire for love, even if it was artificial, began to rise.

That next semester I found myself with several different men and women. If I was in a relationship, my sexual desire was being fed, but if I felt my partner was cheating on me, I would find myself in another person's, bed, car, or hotel room. Shortly into my junior year, I found out what a novelty store was and purchased my first adult toy. I thought this would quench my sexual desire. Although I was masturbating several times a day, I was still craving to be with someone else. It was merely a temporary fix, because I still yearned for the touch of another person. From the age of seven to the age of 23, I slept with over 100 people. I fell into deep depression as the number grew. I couldn't stop.

If These Walls Could Talk

Still on the search for love, I joined a dating site. I met a white man who claimed he was a doctor. We had only had a few conversations before we met at a nearby restaurant. There was something off about him. Everything that he had told me in our previous conversations didn't match what I saw. Physically, he was what he wanted me to see, but when I looked in his eyes, I saw something else. His spirit was off. His eyes looked dark, as if something else was possessing him. You would think that after our date, I would have cut him off, but I didn't. Rent was coming due, and I allowed for him to come over. That night, we had sex, and he was angry that I wanted to use a condom and didn't want to perform oral sex on him. He left and told me that there would be no next time if I didn't want to do things his way. When he left, I blocked his number and never heard from him again.

Shortly after, I found out I was pregnant with my daughter. Even though I never wanted children and knew that my current environment was no place to raise a child, I knew that this would be the first time that I had a chance at real love with no strings attached. I finally realized that if I didn't stop, I was going to end up dead or with a disease that I couldn't get rid of. The love that I was looking for was never going to be found with a man or woman. The love that I was searching for had to come from within me. I had to understand that through the many dangerous acts of sex, God continued to spare me with a clean bill of health. Where many women and men who have sex for the first time end up with a sexually transmitted infection, God continued to shed his grace and mercy over my life. I will not say that since I've had my daughter that I have been celibate, but I will say that I am more cautious of to whom and where I give myself. I will say that I am more into pleasing God and what His thoughts are towards my behavior.

After having my daughter, I still hadn't dealt with my inner battle of being alone. Sex was no longer consuming me, but I wasn't married, I didn't have a stable job, and I felt isolated and without help to raise my child. I was a single mother, just like my mother and her mother. I was battling generational curses that I swore to myself that I wouldn't have to face because I knew better than them.

In 2014, I was admitted to Brookwood Hospital after trying to commit suicide for the fifth time in my life. I stayed there for three days and four nights. I tried my best to convince my psychiatrist that there wasn't anything wrong with me, but he saw through my act and told me that if I didn't admit I had a problem, he would extend my stay. While admitted, I was diagnosed with bipolar depression. I was prescribed six different medications; I felt like a zombie walking earth when I was medicated. I was only discharged under the assumption that I would seek therapy. I did for a little while, but like many people, I was still in denial that I had a real problem. But I also knew that I couldn't go on with my reckless behavior. After several months of therapy, my therapist made me realize that the trauma I'd encounter at an early age set the tone of my bipolar depression. My psychiatrist made me understand that when I was in a manic state, I would go on sex adventures, but once I leveled back off, I would become depressed about my actions.

It has taken me several years to admit I had a problem with sex, but I can honestly say that God is a healer. He spared my life time and time again. When the nights get long and I am feeling lonely, I look to God and know that no matter what people may say about my situation, I have purpose. I know that in this season of my life, God has me alone so that he can get more out of and through me. I know there are still areas in my life in which I need to grow, and that's okay.

God has allowed for me to inspire and give hope to little girls and women who feel as if they've been forgotten; and for that, I will be forever grateful.

Sources

Songwriters: Aaron Kleinstub / Jonathan Bellion / Robyn Fenty / Bleta Rexha / Marshall Mathers / Bryan Fryzel / Maki Athanasiou.

The Monster lyrics © Sony/ATV Music Publishing LLC, Universal Music Publishing Group, Reach Music Ramsay, William M. "Galatia," International Standard Bible Encyclopedia. Edited by James Orr. Publishing, BMG Rights Management US, LLC.

Resources:

National Council on Alcoholism and Drug Dependency – 1-800-622-2255 or https://www.ncadd.org/get-help/get-immediate-help .

Mental Health First Aid https://www.mentalhealth-firstaid.org/ .

Statistics. (n.d.). Retrieved July 10, 2018, from http://www.thehotline.org/resources/statistics/

Adult Bullying. (2015, July 07). Retrieved from http://www.bullyingstatistics.org/content/adult-bullying.html

Bible Versions:

Unless otherwise indicated, scripture quotations are from the Holy Bible, King James Version. All rights reserved.

Scriptures marked NIV are taken from the New International Version®. Copyright © 1973, 1978, 1984, 2011 by Biblica, Inc.™. All rights reserved.

Scriptures marked NKJV are taken from the New King James Version®. Copyright © 1982 by Thomas Nelson. All rights reserved.

Scriptures marked NLT are taken from the New Living Translation®. Copyright © 1996, 2004, 2007, 2013 by Tyndale House Foundation. All rights reserved.

Meet the Authors

Victoria Necole is a mother, daughter, entrepreneur, bestselling author, and confidence coach. She's the owner of the non-profit organization, The Confessions of a Lady, established in August of 2015, where she speaks out against domestic violence, concentrating on those girls seven and older who have been molested and or raped. She is the former owner of the small business boutique, Delani's, established in September of 2013. She is also the co-owner alongside her eight-year-old daughter, Kaytlyn "Delani," of Kaytlyn & Co.—a mommy and me monthly subscription box curated to build love, compassion, and a little sass to an unbreakable bond between mothers and daughters of color.

She is a victor against domestic violence, sexual abuse, and multiple suicide attempts. Victoria understands and knows that through her many trials and tribulations, God has allowed her survive to

About the Authors

spread the message of "your imperfections make you perfect; you're imperfectly perfect," based upon Psalms 139:19.

Victoria is the visionary of *The Waiting Room*, the author of *Ten Ways to Cope with Depression* and *The Girl who Died at 7* and co-author of the bestselling *The Comeback*, with a foreword written by the Grammy-nominated, Dove award-winning Hellen Baylor.

To learn more about the author, visit victorianlong.com or kaytlynandco.com.

Miyoka Chehron is first and foremost a mother of two amazing children, Theresa Michell Johnson and Anton Deshay Johnson. She attempts to be a writer secondly. Born and raised in beautiful Birmingham, Alabama (The Magic City), there has never been anything that she didn't think she could do or achieve. She has had a very successful career in property management for several years and is now ready to take her place in the literary world. She is an avid reader and loves to write in her spare time. She has served in ministry for several years. She is a prophet, minister of music, credit repair specialist, and lifestyle motivator.

About the Authors

Brittaney Pleasant is a wife, mother of four, daughter, author, nurse, birth doula, relationship coach, and photographer. She is the owner of The Love Doula: Childbirth and Coaching Services and of Dreams to Reality Photography. She is also the author of *Break Every Chain: Powerful Prayers to Cover Your Husband*. Brittaney is a survivor of domestic violence and a domestic violence prevention advocate. She is passionate about serving women in her community by helping them to understand the importance of self-love and fostering healthy relationships. Brittaney also has a passion for God and sharing His love with everyone with whom she comes in contact because she understands how it feels to experience His love when we have forgotten to how to love ourselves. She hopes to continue to be a source of inspiration and a glimpse of God to everyone she meets.

To connect, visit her website at
www.thelovedoula.com or email her at
info@thelovedoula.com

LaShun Stewart-Thrasher is a 45-year-old African American female born in Muncie, Indiana and raised in Anderson. She moved back to Muncie in seventh grade and graduated from Muncie South Side High School. She attended Ivy Tech State College where she studied Business Management/HMS, but she didn't graduate because she was put on bed rest due to her pregnancy. She is the oldest child of 11 children has three beautiful children of her own—one daughter and two teenage boys whom she loves so much. They are her world and always keep a smile on her face. She is married, but separated from her husband of eight and a half years (with whom she was together for 13.5 years). Growing up, she suffered various forms of abuse that left her scared and suffering from depression and suicidal thoughts. She is now saved and healed in the name of Jesus.

To connect, email her at
lashunthrasher1@gmail.com

About the Authors

Lola Sterling is a vibrant woman of God who carries the wisdom and fire of the Holy Spirit. Lola loves the presence of God and is a healing voice and example of love to many.

Her teaching style is authentic and aimed at the heart, having been built on her personal testimony of God's incredible goodness and miraculous display in her life and the lives of those that she whispers in the ear of.

She shares her life with her wonderful fiancé Kenneth Tinsley, her six cubs (children), and her three grands. Her four youngest cubs live at home and dearly love and continuously support her in her dreams and her pursuit of Abba. They are the twinkle in her eyes, separate hearts with one beat.

Lola graduated from E.E. Smith in North Carolina and attended F.T.C.C. for Adult and Childhood Education and Development.

Connect with Lola by emailing her at
uniquelymels3@gmail.com

If These Walls Could Talk

Kenyetta Cheatum was born on May 7, 1980 to the late Mrs. Mae Jewel Wade and Robert Cheatum of Tuscaloosa, Alabama. She is their only child. She's married to Samuel E. Wells Jr. and is the mother of two daughters (Tatyianna Wells and Arianna Jones). She graduated from Tuscaloosa County High School in 1998. After graduating high school, she attended Shelton State Community College, where she received a Certificate in Cosmetology. She also attended University of South Alabama's EMT-Basic program. She is currently attending University of Phoenix's Associate of Business program and anticipates graduating on June 25, 2018. She is an Eastern Star of Wrights Choice #696 and the CEO of Big Sistas w/ Purpose LLC. She is the formal Ms. (2015) and Mrs. Tuscaloosa Plus America 2017. In 2017, she was awarded the "Footprints in the City" award.

To connect, email her at
kenyetta.cheatum@yahoo.com

About the Authors

Kerscelia L. Patterson is a collaborator, mentor, advocate, entrepreneur, ally, and graduate student. She is a wife and mom being renewed by the power of the gospel. She holds a Bachelor's of Arts in Psychology and a Bachelor's of Science in Criminal Justice. Certified Youth Mental Health First Aid Instructor and is currently pursuing a Master's degree in Health Administration at the University of Southern Indiana. She assisted in launching the first-ever certified nursing assistant program at an alternative high school in Vanderburgh County, providing jobs to some medically under-served populations. She is a co-creator of a local television network designed to improve quality health care in rural and medically underserved areas in our region and to provide resources for the community. Kerscelia is honored to serve as president of the Women of Color in the Academy and Equity, Diversity, and Inclusion Councils at the University of Southern Indiana.

Star Washington—a wife, mom, sister, and friend—is an inspiration to her generation. She is a history-making business owner. Star is the first African American to independently own a weight loss clinic in Birmingham, Alabama. She is the owner of SlimFit Weight Loss Clinics. She is also the founder of Luxe Life University, where she helps new and aspiring business owners go from vision to reality despite their circumstances. Star is also a motivational speaker and bestselling author. Over the years, she has been a very instrumental part in the opening of businesses of many of her peers. Her motto is "helping the everyday woman take life circumstances and use them to their advantage to make their dreams a reality." She believes that empowering women with motivation as well as business knowledge allows them to be able to properly execute their vision. Between building a weight loss empire and helping others achieve their dreams, Star is a powerhouse in her industry. Her goal is to change her generation one dream at a time! "Success is a choice, and I chose success!"

Learn more at
www.iamstarwashington.com

About the Authors

Shaniqua Davis is a recent graduate of law school and a soon-to-be attorney. She was born in Queens, New York, was raised in Prattville, Alabama, and currently resides in Birmingham, Alabama with her fiancé. She has a dog named Onyx who has been a loyal part of the family for 11 years. Shaniqua enjoys reading, but never imagined writing about herself. In fact, it has always been one of her weaknesses.

Shaniqua's goals in life are simple: to leave a lasting impression in the legal field, be successful, spend as much time with family and friends as possible, and raise a beautiful family. Her determination and strong will has allowed her to overcome many obstacles in life and always press forward.

Connect with me via email
shaniqua.davis2@gmail.com

Melissa Morehead is a woman of God, passionate speaker, community servant leader, and mentor. Alongside working with Social Security Administration, she is also co-host of Community Chat, 98.5FM-WEOA. She is a CASA Volunteer, Legal Aid Society of Evansville Board Member, Leadership Evansville Alumna, and the Operations Director Leader for Girl Scouts of Evansville, Troop 766. Melissa is a veteran of the United States Navy and is the mother of three adult children, the god-mother of one, and grandmother of one. She is the 2017-2018 recipient of the UEAAA Mentor of the Year award. She holds a Bachelor of Science in Global Leadership Development. When she is not working or serving the community, she is active at her place of worship, Victory Temple, COGIC, under the leadership of Superintendent Levar St. Germain and Lady Elect Andrea. She currently resides in Evansville, Indiana.

To connect, email her at
moore.melissa93@yahoo.com

About the Authors

Jamie Oliver is a vibrant single mother of three children—D'Wonte, Diamond, and Destiny. She was born to James E. Oliver and Annie Wilson Oliver on September 30, 1981 in Fairfield, Alabama. She grew up in the small-town of Brighton, Alabama. She graduated from Midfield High School in 1999. She has an Associate's degree in Computer Information Systems and Administrative Office Management. Ms. Oliver is the owner of Sensational Taste Cakes N Things, The Destination Is Yours Travel Agency, and All Dolled Up Hair Braiding. She is a member of the Prince Hall Chapter of the Order of Eastern Star and the Black Girls Run running group. Her passion is to network with young girls and women through reading inspirational books; therefore, in 2015 she founded the Graced For This book club. Ms. Oliver is now working with young girls and women to continue to bring awareness of domestic violence and preventive ways to stop this disease that plagues all communities.

Contact her at
FacttoFace18@gmail.com

CREATING DISTINCTIVE BOOKS WITH INTENTIONAL RESULTS

We're a collaborative group of creative masterminds with a mission to produce high-quality books to position you for monumental success in the marketplace.

Our professional team of writers, editors, designers, and marketing strategists work closely together to ensure that every detail of your book is a clear representation of the message in your writing.

Want to know more?
Write to us at info@publishyourgift.com
or call (888) 949-6228

Discover great books, exclusive offers, and more at
www.PublishYourGift.com

Connect with us on social media

@publishyourgift

www.ingramcontent.com/pod-product-compliance
Lightning Source LLC
Chambersburg PA
CBHW052146110526
44591CB00012B/1881